The Source

Budgeting, Credit, & Housing

I0426882

Copyright © 2014 by Purin Williams

All rights reserved. No part of this publication may be reproduced, distributed, or transmitted in any form or by any means, including photocopying, recording, or other electronic or mechanical methods, without the prior written permission of the publisher, except in the case of brief quotations embodied in critical reviews and certain other noncommercial uses permitted by copyright law. For permission requests, write to the publisher, addressed "Attention: Permissions Coordinator," at the address below.

Williams Commercial Group, LLC

PO Box 2075

Broken Arrow, OK 74013

Ordering Information:

Quantity sales. Special discounts are available on quantity purchases by corporations, associations, and others.

For details, contact the publisher at the address above.

Orders by U.S. trade bookstores and wholesalers.

Call:

(888)654-3129

or visit

www.williamsrealty.org

ISBN 978-1-312-59101-1

9 781312 591011

CONTENTS

Introduction 4

Chapter 1 Pros &cons of homeownership..............................5

  Handouts: 5

  Buying a Home 5

  Pros & Cons...6

Chapter 2 Budgets...7

  Handouts: 7

  Budget Basics 7

    How can we help you today? 7

  Goal Setting and Money Management......................8

    Debt Ratio Example: 8

Chapter 3 Credit 11

  Handouts: 11

  Pre-Qualification and Loan-Worthiness 11

  Credit Repair and Debt Repayment........................11

    Three Credit Bureaus' Phone Numbers & Addresses 12

Chapter 4 Housing...13

  Handouts: 13

  Down Payment, Closing Cost and Moving Expense 13

    Shopping for a Home 13

    Make an Offer 13

    Inspections...14

  Insurances 14

Chapter 5 Mortgage Variables & Refinancing.....................16

  Handouts: 16

  When Shopping for a Mortgage 16

    REFINANCING 16

    TITLE AND DEED SCAMS 17

    Mortgage Transfers..17

  Mortgage 101..17

Option 1: Fixed vs. Adjustable-Rate..17

Option 2: Government-Insured vs. Conventional Loans 18

Option 3: Jumbo vs. Conforming Loan...19

Option 4: Real Estate Purchase Options 19

Principal, Interest, Taxes & Insurance 20

Chapter 6 Contract Overview...21

Handouts: 21

Realestate Contract 21

AVOIDING DELINQUENCY/PRIORITY OF HOUSE PAYMENT.............................23

HOME Maintenance..23

What Consumers Need to Know About the Fair Housing Act 25

Protection if You Have a Disability 26

Contact your Local Office..32

Real Estate terms 33

INTRODUCTION

When you reach the point where you are considering renting or buying real estate, you need to know your rights. You also need to know your obligations. You need to be familiar with some of the terms that are used in real estate dealings. You need to know about the companies and laws that can be helpful to you as you deal in real estate.

During your adult life you can expect to spend about 25% of all your earnings for housing. This may be in the form of rent or it may be payments on a home you are buying. Since such a large part of your budget will be spent on housing, you want to be sure that you are getting the best buy for your money. You need to know what you are signing as you sign a lease for an apartment or a contract to purchase a house. In short, the more you know about real estate dealings the better off you will be when the day comes for you to rent or buy real estate.

When choosing among housing options, there are many decisions you must make. Should you rent or buy? If you buy, what sort of financing should you choose, and what type of mortgage is best for you? The U.S. Department of Housing and Urban Development (HUD) funds housing counseling agencies throughout the country to help you make these decisions. These organizations can give you advice on buying a home, renting, defaults, foreclosures, credit issues, and reverse mortgages. To contact the agency nearest you, call 1-800-569-4287 or visit www. hud.gov. Homeowners with problems that could result in default on their mortgage or foreclosure on their property are encouraged to immediately contact a HUD-approved housing counseling agency.

If you believe you are being discriminated against during your housing search because of your race, color, nationality, religion, sex, familial status, or disability, contact HUD's Office of Fair Housing and Equal Opportunity.

CHAPTER 1 PROS &CONS OF HOMEOWNERSHIP

The Basics
MLS Listing

Buying a Home

Buying a home is one of the most complex financial decisions you will ever make. In addition to the financial and legal issues involved, real estate agents and lenders may not be acting in your best interest.

- Real estate agents represent the seller, not the buyer. Consider hiring a buyer's agent who works for you, not for the seller.
- Get prices on other homes. Knowing the price of other homes in a neighborhood will help you avoid paying too much.
- Have the property inspected. Use a licensed home inspector to inspect the property carefully before you agree to buy it.
- Check to see if a particular home requires you to pay any.
- Ongoing homeowner's association or condo fees.

You will probably live in a number of apartments and houses during your life. Each time you make a housing move you will draw upon the information that you will gain from this booklet. Among other things, you will learn:

- Homeownership Pros and Cons
- Budget
- Goal Setting and Money Management
- Pre-Qualifying and Loan-Worthiness
- Credit Repair and Debt Repayment Options
- Down Payment, Closing Costs and Moving Expenses
- Saving Techniques
- Principal and Interest/Tax and Insurance PITI
- Purchase Options
- Mortgage Variables
- Insurances
- Purchase Process
- Avoiding Delinquency/Priority of House Payment
- Home Maintenance
- Refinancing

Pros	Cons
+ Pride of ownership	+ Location
+ Appreciation Potential	+ Responsibility of ownership
+ Tax Deduction	+ Risk of having to sell at the
+ Hedge Against Inflation	wrong time
+ Helps Build Good Credit	+ Down Payment, Closing
+ Remodel Flexible	Cost and Earnest Money
(Maintenance Etc.)	+ Long-Term Commitment
+ Flexibility to have pets, a	+ Increased Expense (Yard,
garden, commitments to	Utilities, Repairs, HOA,
make noise	Lifestyle Change)
+ Storage space/Garage	+ Lack of Amenities

CHAPTER 2 BUDGETS

Monthly Income
Monthly Expense
Monthly Discretionary Income
Monthly Spending Plan

Budget Basics

Budgets are used to determine where you are and to help you develop a plan to take you where you want to be.

Financial goals are started by establishing challenging but attainable financial goals for your family.

Develop a budget that utilizes no more than 36 to 45% of your income toward your overall monthly debt.

As you increase your income add the additional income towards needed purchases such as: transportation, savings, debt elimination, and eventually home purchase.

Use a goal setting calendar to develop practical financial goals that fit your family's desires.

How can we help you today?

- ☐ Transportation
- ☐ Savings (Vacation, Kids College, Retirement)
- ☐ Debt Elimination
- ☐ Home Purchase
- ☐ _____
- ☐ _____

Decide what kind of home you want and need. Determine your housing needs and wants according to your affordability before you go shopping.

Practical things you can do while you're deciding.

1. Know your score
2. Have any negative items removed that have been paid
3. Locate any errors and have those removed as well
4. Make sure your total debts (credit report only)/income is below 46% including what you feel comfortable paying every month on house payment
5. Also most lenders require you to be on your job for at least 2 years or provide reasonable explanation for 2 year gap
   a. In school for year 1 and in currently working for 1 year in same field.
   b. Change careers but doing same kind of work.

Debt Ratio Example:

	Expense		Income
New Mortgage	700	Salary	2500
Car	200	Child Support	500
Credit Cards	100		
Student Loans	50		
	1050		3000
		Debts ÷	1050
		Income	3000
			0.35

To manage your money wisely, set financial goals and establish a budget to achieve your goals. Financial goals are statements about things you wish you could afford. For example, you may have a goal to establish an emergency savings fund of $2,000 by the end of the year.

What are your personal financial goals? If you had $2,000, what would you do with it? Would you invest it in your business? Would you buy a car?

You will be able to accomplish these goals if you manage your finances and put money aside on a regular basis. The key is setting financial goals that are **Specific, Measurable, Attainable, Realistic,** and **Trackable** (**SMART**):

- **Specific.** State exactly what you want to achieve, how you're going to do it, and when you want to achieve it. For example:
  General Goal Statement: I want to improve my finances.
  Specific Goal Statement: I want to pay off my medical bill in 8 months by negotiating a payment plan with my doctor.
- **Measurable.** A goal should be measurable so you know when you have achieved it.
  General Goal Statement: I will pay off most of my credit card debt soon.
  Measurable Goal Statement: In the next six months, I will pay three of my five credit card bills in full.
- **Attainable.** Make sure the goal is within reasonable reach.
  General Goal Statement: I will save money.
  Attainable Goal Statement: I will save $1,000 in a year by putting aside $3 each day.
- **Realistic.** Is the goal realistic for you? Don't ignore your limitations. Your goals need to be tasks that you can reasonably accomplish. *General Goal Statement:* By managing my money well, next year I will become a millionaire.

9

Realistic Goal Statement: By managing my money well, next year I will be debt free and will have an emergency fund equal to three months of living expenses.

- **Trackable.** Being able to track your progress encourages you to keep going and reach your goal.

  General Goal Statement: I will increase my savings goal every year.

  Trackable Statement: Each year I will save 10 percent more than the previous year.

CHAPTER 3 CREDIT

Good Faith Estimate

Pre-Qualification and Loan-Worthiness

Apply for a mortgage loan. Once you choose a lender and a loan program, you will complete a formal application at the lender's office.

Lender Conversations

Most lenders will tell you if they have a loan that fits your criteria based on you providing the following information.

- ☐ Source of Closing Cost (seller, borrowed, 401k)
- ☐ Source and amount of Down Payment (Will you finance 100% of the home price)
- ☐ Have you filed bankruptcy within the last 2 years
- ☐ Credit Score
- ☐ Monthly Income
- ☐ Monthly Expense

Credit Repair and Debt Repayment

The 3 major credit bureaus in the United States are Equifax, Experian and TransUnion. There are several likely reasons why you might need to contact one of these credit reporting agencies.	dispute an item on one of your credit reports, check the status of an existing report, order an updated credit report
	place a fraud alert on your credit profile,
	place a security freeze on your file, sign-up for credit monitoring,
	inquire about other personal services and business solutionsIt is important to contact each company if you are having credit issue or concerns, or simply want to be proactive by monitoring your credit profile.

Contact Information:

Equifax
www.Equifax.com
P.O. Box 740256, Atlanta, Georgia 30374
1-800-685-1111: Inquiries 1-888-766-0008:

Experian
www.Experian.com
P.O. Box 9554, Allen, Texas 75013
1-888-397-3742: 1-877-284-7942:

Transunion
www.TransUnion.com
P.O. Box 6790, Fullerton, CA 92834
1-800-493-2392: 1-800-888-4213:

CHAPTER 4 HOUSING

Handouts:
Insurance Quote

Down Payment, Closing Cost and Moving Expense
You Need To Know:

Earnest money:	• Typically $1,000 to $1500. • When developing your savings goal it's important to remember this number.
Down-Payments:	• Vary depending on the type of loan you receive. • Example: Some banks offer 1st time home-buyer loans that are 100% financing. This simple means you pay earnest money and closing cost only.
Closing Cost:	• Fees charged by the lender, Title Company, and Inspection Company. • Ttypically 7% of Purchase Price. • Example: Purchase Price: $100,000 * 7% = $7000. These fees can be obtained from many sources: The seller and home purchase programs.

Shopping for a Home
Shop for a home. You may choose to work with a real estate agent to help you more easily find a home that fits your needs and your budget. Take your time, take notes and ask questions and narrow your search by looking carefully at property conditions, neighborhood qualities, and community services.

Make an Offer
Make an offer. When you finally find a house in your price range and decide what you are willing to pay for it, you will make an offer, or a written purchase proposal. An offer is usually accompanied by earnest money to show your intention to complete the sale.

Get a professional home inspection. Once your offer is accepted, hire a professional home inspector to check the structural soundness of your property. If you made your purchase contract contingent on a satisfactory home inspection, you have options to address any problems with the house before you have to live with them. If the inspection shows major problems, you can cancel the sale and get your earnest money back. Or you can ask the seller to either make the repairs or give you a credit for the amount it would cost you to make them.

Obtain insurance and have additional inspections. You will have to shop for and buy homeowner's insurance to protect against losses that result from damage to your home or liability.

You may be able to save hundreds of dollars a year on homeowners insurance by shopping around. You can also save money by following these tips:

- Consider a higher deductible. Increasing your deductible by just a few hundred dollars can make a big difference in your premiums.

- Ask your insurance agent about discounts. You may be able to get a lower premium if your home has safety features such as dead-bolt locks, smoke detectors, an alarm system, storm shutters, or fire-retardant roofing material. Persons over 55 years of age or long-term customers may also be offered discounts.
- Insure your house, NOT the land under it. After a disaster, the land is still there. If you do not subtract the value of the land when deciding how much homeowners insurance to buy, you will pay more than you should.
- Make certain you purchase enough coverage to replace what is insured. "Replacement" coverage gives you the money to rebuild your home and replace its contents. An "Actual Cash Value" policy is cheaper but pays the difference between your property's worth at the time of loss minus depreciation for age and wear.
- Ask about any special coverage you might need. You may have to pay extra for computers, cameras, jewelry, art, antiques, musical instruments, stamp collections, etc.

- Remember that flood and earthquake damage are not covered by a standard homeowners policy. The cost of a separate earthquake policy will depend on the likelihood of earthquakes in your area. Homeowners who live in areas prone to flooding should take advantage of the National Flood Insurance Program.
- If you are a renter, do not assume your landlord carries insurance on your personal belongings. Purchase a separate policy for renters.
- Remember that flood and earthquake damage are not covered by a standard homeowners policy. The cost of a separate earthquake policy will depend on the likelihood of earthquakes in your area. Homeowners who live in areas prone to flooding should take advantage of the National Flood Insurance Program.
- If you are a renter, do not assume your landlord carries insurance on your personal belongings. Purchase a separate policy for renters.

Step 7: Close the loan. The final step in the home purchase process is called the closing, or settlement. This is when the closing documents are signed, closing costs are paid, and the house keys are given to the new owner. It's time to move in!

CHAPTER 5 MORTGAGE VARIABLES & REFINANCING

Handouts:

Settlement Statement
Mortgage
Federal Truth & Lending
Grant Deed

When Shopping for a Mortgage

When shopping for a home mortgage, make sure you obtain all of the relevant information:

- Research current interest rates. Check the real estate section of your local newspaper, use the Internet, or call several lenders for information.
- Check the rates for 15-year, 20-year, and 30-year mortgages. You may be able to save thousands of dollars in interest charges by getting the shortest-term mortgage you can afford.
- Ask for details on the same loan amount, loan term, and type of loan from multiple lenders so you can compare the information. Be sure to get the APR, which takes into account not only the interest rate, but also points, broker fees, and other credit charges expressed as a yearly rate.
- Ask whether the rate is fixed or adjustable. The interest rate on adjustable-rate mortgages (ARMs) can vary a great deal over the lifetime of the mortgage. An increase of several percentage points might raise payments by hundreds of dollars per month.
- If a loan has an adjustable-rate, ask when and how the rate and loan payment can change.
- Find out how much of a down payment is required. Some lenders require 20% of the home's purchase price as a down payment. But many lenders now offer loans that require less. In these cases, you may be required to purchase private mortgage insurance (PMI) to protect the lender if you fall behind on payments.

REFINANCING

Refinancing your mortgage can help you save money. Some factors that make it a good idea, include:

- A decrease in interest rates.
- A change in the length of your mortgage.

- A change in the type of mortgage (fixed vs adjustable).For an overview, review the Federal Reserve's publication www.federalreserve.gov/pubs/refinancings/default.htm.
- If PMI is required, ask what the total cost of the insurance will be.

TITLE AND DEED SCAMS

Ask whether you can pay off the loan early, and whether there is a penalty for doing so.

There is a long list of sources for mortgage loans: mortgage banks, mortgage brokers, banks, thrifts and credit unions, home builders, real estate agencies, and Internet lenders.

For more information on home buying and mortgages, visit www.hud.gov. Other good sources include the Mortgage Bankers Association at www.homeloanlearningcenter.com and NeighborWorks America's home ownership website at www.keystomyhome.org.

Mortgage Transfers

Mortgage companies must notify you when your loan is sold to another company. The rules ensure that you know who owns your loan, which is important information if you have questions or payment disputes or want to discuss loan modifications. Under these rules, the company that takes over your loan must send you a notice within 30 days of acquiring it. Even with a new loan owner, the company that "services" or handles your loan might not change, and you might continue to send your mortgage payments to the same address. If that loan servicer changes, you will receive a separate notice.

Beware of companies that pressure you into buying a certified copy of your title or deed. You do not have to use a private company to obtain a certified copy of the deed to your home. In many states you can obtain this document from your local Registrar of Deeds for free or at a low cost. Some companies may even State that they are endorsed by the government. Don't believe it; the government does not endorse any company selling these products.
For more information about servicing companies, visit the CFPB's overview at www.consumerfinance.gov/ askcfpb/215/what-happens-if-my-servicer-changes-what- do-i-do.html.

Mortgage 101

There are many different types of mortgages available to home buyers

Option 1: Fixed vs. Adjustable-Rate

- **Fixed-rate** mortgage loans have the same interest rate for the entire repayment term. Because of this, the size of your monthly payment will stay the same, month after month, and year after year. It will never change. This is true even for long-term financing options, such as the 30-year fixed-rate loan. It has the same interest rate, and the same monthly payment, for the entire term.

- **Adjustable-rate** mortgage loans (ARMs) have an interest rate that will change or "adjust" from time to time. Typically, the rate on an ARM will change every year after an initial period of remaining fixed. It is therefore referred to as a "hybrid" product. A hybrid ARM loan is one that starts off with a fixed or unchanging interest rate, before switching over to an adjustable-rate. For instance, the 5/1 ARM loan carries a fixed-rate of interest for the first *five* years, after which it begins to adjust every *one* year, or annually. That's what the five and the one signify in the name.

Option 2: Government-Insured vs. Conventional Loans

So you'll have to choose between a fixed and adjustable-rate type of mortgage, as explained in the previous section. But there are other choices as well. You'll also have to decide whether you want to use a government-insured home loan (such as Federal Housing Administration (FHA) or Veterans Affairs (VA)), or a conventional "regular" type of loan. The differences between these two mortgage types are covered below.

A **conventional** home loan is one that is not insured or guaranteed by the Federal government in any way. This distinguishes it from the three government-backed mortgage types explained below (FHA, VA and United States Department of Agriculture (USDA)).

Government-insured home loans include the following:

FHA Loans

The FHA mortgage insurance program is managed by the Department of HUD, which is a department of the Federal government. FHA loans are available to all types of borrowers, not just first-time buyers. The government insures the lender against losses that might result from borrower default. *Advantage*: This program allows you to make a down payment as low as 3.5% of the purchase price. *Disadvantage*: You'll have to pay for mortgage insurance, which will increase the size of your monthly payments.

VA Loans

The U.S. Department of VA offers a loan program to military service members and their families. Similar to the FHA program, these types of mortgages are guaranteed by the Federal government. This means the VA will reimburse the lender for any losses that may result from borrower default. The primary advantage of this program (and it's a big one) is that borrowers can receive 100%

financing for the purchase of a home. That means no down payment whatsoever.

USDA / Rural Housing Service (RHS) Loans
The USDA offers a loan program for rural borrowers who meet certain income requirements. The program is managed by the RHS, which is part of the Department of Agriculture. This type of mortgage loan is offered to "rural residents who have a steady, low or modest income, and yet are unable to obtain adequate housing through conventional financing." Income must be no higher than 115% of the adjusted area median income [AMI]. The AMI varies by county. See the link below for details.

Option 3: Jumbo vs. Conforming Loan

There is another distinction that needs to be made, and it's based on the *size* of the loan. Depending on the amount you are trying to borrow, you might fall into either the jumbo or conforming category. Here's the difference between these two mortgage types.

- **A conforming loan** is one that meets the underwriting guidelines of Fannie Mae or Freddie Mac, particularly where size is concerned. Fannie and Freddie are the two government-controlled corporations that purchase and sell mortgage-backed securities. Simply put, they buy loans from the lenders who generate them, and then sell them to investors via Wall Street. A conforming loan falls within their maximum size limits, and otherwise "conforms" to pre-established criteria.

A jumbo loan, on the other hand, exceeds the conforming loan limits established by Fannie Mae and Freddie Mac. This type of mortgage represents a higher risk for the lender, mainly due to its size. As a result, jumbo borrowers typically must have excellent credit and larger down payments, when compared to conforming loans. Interest rates are generally higher with the jumbo products, as well.

Option 4: Real Estate Purchase Options

A real estate purchase option can be used to secure real estate property for short periods of time.

Someone who finds an empty lot in a desirable neighborhood may want to purchase it to build a new home. If he does not have funds available to make the purchase at the time, he may buy an option in order to safeguard the lot while he secures further funding. He offers the landowner a small percentage of the purchase price of the lot to secure the option. The option contract will determine the length of time of the option and the purchase price of the plot of land.

The landowner cannot sell the plot to anybody else during the term of the option. At the end of the option term, the landowner must sell the land at the predetermined price, even if land values have risen drastically in the interim. If the buyer has not yet secured funding and cannot buy the land, he forfeits the sum that he paid when buying the option.

Principal, Interest, Taxes & Insurance

When lenders underwrite your loan, they calculate your insurance and property taxes as if they were paid monthly. This calculator does the same thing. Of course, you may have to mentally add mortgage insurance, if required, and Homeowner's Association Fees.

Years:

Interest Rate:

Loan Amount:

CHAPTER 6 CONTRACT OVERVIEW

Sample Contract

Realestate Contract

The pathway to finding that perfect home starts with the home search. You start with your ideal home features such as: general location, bedroom, baths, living spaces, and garage space. Once you determine the maximum criteria inform your Realtor of your minimum budget requirements. If you need the seller to pay closing cost let the Realtor know upfront, assuming the lender allows.

The Realtor should look for homes that meet your criteria in the area that you want to live in. The Realtor will show you properties and discuss options that meet your satisfaction. Once you find the home you love it's time to negotiate the offer.

When negotiating the offer it's important to remember that most sellers are expecting you to ask for certain things and are prepared to put up a fight. A good strategy is to ask for a little more than you're willing to settle for.

The contract begins with THE SALE, naming the parties involved in the sale.

THE PURCHASE PRICE, the price you would like to purchase the property for, this includes the earnest money. The earnest money is given to the seller's Realtor and held an account that will be given back to you at closing. However, once you and the seller agree on the terms of the contract and sign it the earnest money can be taken if you fail to uphold your end of the sale.

When writing an offer the contract will include a section on PERSONAL PROPERTY/FIXTURE. The contract provides that all items that are fixed to the property remain with the property. If you want other items such as, refrigerator, window treatments, or stove, you must write it in this section.

Following is the EFFECTIVE DATES of TIME periods. Simply put, the effective date is the date the contract becomes effective after you agree. The effective date of the contract will also start the 10 DAY RIGHT OF RECESSION and THE TIME FOR INSPECTIONS. The 10 day right of recession means you have 10 days from the contract date to cancel the contract for any reason. Also, the buyer and seller can negotiate a dollar amount that the contract will not cancel in the event the cost of inspections do not exceed a certain dollar amount. The buyer can request the seller to pay this amount. The buyer can specify how many days the seller has to review repair estimate and how many days the seller has to complete the inspections.

The DISCLOSURES AND DISCLAIMERS are perhaps one of the most important part of the contract. The Disclosure is a document were the seller informs you of any defects or major repairs to the property. You should review this before presenting an offer to make sure these items aren't deal breakers. The DISCLAIMERS are from the Realtor or owners of unoccupied properties. They let you know the findings or unknown findings of any defects.

The last part of the contract allows you to make any additional request to the seller, such as: requesting the seller to pay up to a certain amount of your closing cost.

FINANCING terms, you write the percentage of the purchase price will be covered by a loan. For example 100% financing. The financing supplement, states that if the loan falls through and it's not a fault of the buyer the buyer shall receive all earnest back.

The Realtor submits your offer along with earnest money and pre-approval letter to the seller. Negotiations begin and once you agree to the terms your effective dates start:

Complete inspections of all or some of the following items as soon as possible:

➢ Flood, Storm, Run off Water, Storm Sewer Backup or Water History- the seller discloses whether the home is located in flood zone.
➢ Psychologically Impacted Property- the seller discloses whether certain events or circumstances have occurred on the property that might create emotional or psychological disturbances. Example: the home was meth lab or death occurred on property.
➢ Megan's Law- Buyer can obtain a list of sex offenders in the area from law enforcement.
➢ Hazard Insurance- Buyer should obtain a commitment of hazard insurance but the contract shall State the seller is responsible for the property until title is transferred into the buyer's name.
➢ Environmental Risks- it is the buyer responsibility to find out about lead based paint, mold, asbestos, methamphetamine, or other toxic materials.
➢ Roof Inspections- most insurance companies require it.
➢ Structural – include square footage and prior structural work.
➢ Fixtures Equipment & Systems- mechanical parts of the home such as Jacuzzi's, ceiling fans, heating and air, fireplaces, and etc.
➢ Wood Destroying Organisms- such as termites and ants.

After inspections are complete your Realtor will submit the cost of any repairs from the inspection company and submit to selling broker. The buyer will either accept or reject your request for repairs to be completed. You can also request to cancel the contract.

Title and Closing

The title company will have mortgage inspection, Title Examination, Title Examination, Survey, and Title Insurance completed on your behalf. It is best to wait until you agree on inspections before starting this process. Inspections cost (typically $1000) and Title charges ($1200) are your responsibility until you close the loan unless the seller failed to disclose.

AVOIDING DELINQUENCY/PRIORITY OF HOUSE PAYMENT

If you miss your mortgage payments, foreclosure may occur. This is the legal means your lender can use to repossess your home. If you owe more than your property is worth, a deficiency judgment is pursued. A deficiency judgment would require you to pay the difference between the amount you owe and your home's value. Both foreclosures and deficiency judgments have a negative impact on your credit history.

These steps can help:

- Do not ignore letters from your lender. If you are having problems making your payments, call or write to your lender's Loss Mitigation Department immediately. Explain your situation. Be prepared to provide financial information, such as your monthly income and expenses. Without this information, the lender may not be able to help you.
- Stay in your home for now; you may not qualify for assistance if you abandon your property.
- Contact a HUD-approved housing counselor. Call 1-800-569-4287 or TDD 1-800-877-8339 for the housing counseling agency nearest you. These agencies are valuable resources.
- Contact Making Home Affordable for help. Call 1-888-995-4673, or 1-877-304-9709 for hearing-impaired homeowners, to talk to a HUD-approved credit counselor who will guide you through your options for free.
- HUD counselors frequently have information on services and programs offered by government agencies as well as private and community organizations that could help you. The housing counseling agency may also offer credit counseling. These services are usually free of charge.

For more information, contact The U.S. Department of HUD.

HOME Maintenance

Home improvements and repairs can cost thousands of dollars and are the subject of frequent complaints.

When selecting a contractor:

- Get recommendations and references. Talk to friends, family, and others who have used the contractor for similar work.
- Get at least three written estimates. Insist the contractors come to your home to evaluate what needs to be done. Be sure the estimates are based on the same work so you can make meaningful comparisons.
- Check contractor complaint records with your State or local consumer protection agency or the Better Business Bureau.
- Make sure the contractor meets licensing and registration requirements. Your State or local consumer protection agency can help you determine the necessary requirements.
- Get the names of suppliers and ask them whether the contractor makes timely payments.
- Contact your local building inspection department to check for permit and inspection requirements. Be wary if the contractor asks you to get the permit; it could mean the firm is not licensed.
- Be sure your contractor is insured. The contractor should have personal liability, property damage, and workers' compensation insurance for workers and subcontractors. Also check with your insurance company to find out whether you are covered for any injury or damage that might occur.
- Insist on a written contract that states exactly what work will be done, the quality of materials that will be used, warranties, timetables, the names of any subcontractors, the total price of the job, and the schedule of payments.
- Try to limit your down payment. Some states have laws limiting the amount of down payment required.
- Understand your payment options. Compare the cost of getting your own loan versus contractor financing.
- Don't make a final payment or sign a final release until you are satisfied with the work and know that subcontractors and suppliers have been paid. Some State laws allow unpaid subcontractors and suppliers to put a lien on your home for bills the contractor failed to pay.
- Pay by credit card when you can. You may have the right to withhold payment to the credit card company until problems are corrected.

Be especially cautious if the contractor:

- Comes door-to-door or seeks you out.
- Happens to have material left over from a recent job.
- Offers you discounts for finding other customers.
- Quotes a price that is out of line with other estimates.
- Pressures you for an immediate decision.
- Can only be reached by leaving messages with an answering service.

- Has no physical address for the business.
- Has out-of-State license plates.
- Asks you to pay for the entire job up front.

With most home improvements, Federal law gives you three business days to cancel without penalty. Of course, you would be liable for any benefit already received. State laws may also provide some protection. And remember, if you finance home improvements with a home equity loan and do not make your payments, you could lose your home.

What Consumers Need to Know About the Fair Housing Act

When you apply for housing, you cannot be discriminated against based on you're:

- Race
- Color
- Religion
- National origin
- Sex
- Familial status, or
- Disability.

Know your rights violated?

Has anyone taken any of the following actions based on race, color, religion, national origin, sex, familial status, or disability:·

- ☐ Refuse to rent or sell housing
- ☐ Refuse to negotiate for housing
- ☐ Set different terms, conditions, or privileges for sale/rental of a dwelling
- ☐ Falsely deny that housing is available for inspection, sale, or rental
- ☐ Deny anyone access to or membership in a facility or service related to the sale or rental of housing
- ☐ Refuse to make a mortgage loan or discriminate in appraising property
- ☐ Refuse to provide information regarding loans
- ☐ Impose different terms or conditions on a loan
- ☐ Threaten, coerce, intimidate, or interfere with anyone exercising a fair housing right or assisting others who exercise that right
- ☐ Advertise or make any statement that indicates a limitation or preference based on those characteristics. (This particular prohibition applies to single-family and owner-occupied housing that is otherwise not controlled by the Fair Housing Act)

If you answer "yes" to any of the questions above, consider filing a complaint at the numbers below.

Protection if You Have a Disability

If you or someone associated with you:

Have a physical or mental disability (including hearing, mobility and visual impairments, chronic alcoholism, chronic mental illness, AIDS, AIDS Related Complex and mental retardation) that substantially limits one or more major life activities

Have a record of such a disability or are regarded as having such a disability
Your landlord may not:

- Refuse to let you make reasonable modifications to your dwelling or common use areas, at your expense, if necessary for the disabled person to use the housing. (Where reasonable, the landlord may permit changes only if you agree to restore the property to its original condition when you move.)
- Refuse to make reasonable accommodations in rules, policies, practices or services if necessary for the disabled person to use the housing.

Example: A building with a no pet's policy must allow a visually impaired tenant to keep a guide dog.

Example: An apartment complex that offers tenants ample, unassigned parking must honor a request from a mobility-impaired tenant for a reserved space near her apartment if necessary to assure that she can have access to her apartment.

However, housing need not be made available to a person who is a direct threat to the health or safety of others or who currently uses illegal drugs.

In the Sale and Rental of Housing:

No one may take any of the following actions based on race, color, national origin, religion, sex, familial status or handicap:

- Refuse to rent or sell housing
- Refuse to negotiate for housing
- Make housing unavailable
- Deny a dwelling
- Set different terms, conditions or privileges for sale or rental of a dwelling
- Provide different housing services or facilities
- Falsely deny that housing is available for inspection, sale, or rental
- For profit, persuade owners to sell or rent (blockbusting)

26

- ☐ Deny anyone access to or membership in a facility or service (such as a multiple listing service) related to the sale or rental of housing
- ☐ In Mortgage Lending: No one may take any of the following actions based on race, color, national origin, religion, sex, familial status or handicap (disability):

Refuse to make a mortgage loan

- ☐ Refuse to provide information regarding loans
- ☐ Impose different terms or conditions on a loan, such as different interest rates, points, or fees
- ☐ Discriminate in appraising property
- ☐ Refuse to purchase a loan
- ☐ Set different terms or conditions for purchasing a loan
- ☐ In Addition: It is illegal for anyone to:
- ☐ Threaten, coerce, intimidate or interfere with anyone exercising a fair housing right or assisting others who exercise that right
- ☐ Advertise or make any statement that indicates a limitation or preference based on race, color, national origin, religion, sex, familial status, or handicap. This prohibition against discriminatory advertising applies to single-family and owner-occupied housing that is otherwise exempt from the Fair Housing Act
- ☐ Requirements for New Buildings

In buildings that are ready for first occupancy after March 13, 1991, and have an elevator and four or more units:

- ☐ Public and common areas must be accessible to persons with disabilities
- ☐ Doors and hallways must be wide enough for wheelchairs
- ☐ All units must have:
- ☐ An accessible route into and through the unit
- ☐ Accessible light switches, electrical outlets, thermostats and other environmental controls
- ☐ Reinforced bathroom walls to allow later installation of grab bars Kitchens and bathrooms that can be used by people in wheelchairs
- ☐ If a building with four or more units has no elevator and will be ready for first occupancy after March 13, 1991, these standards apply to ground floor units
- ☐ These requirements for new buildings do not replace any more stringent standards in State or local law

Housing Opportunities for Families

Unless a building or community qualifies as housing for older persons, it may not discriminate based on familial status. That is, it may not discriminate against families in which one or more children under 18 live with:

- ☐ A parent
- ☐ A person who has legal custody of the child or children
- ☐ The designee of the parent or legal custodian, with the parent or custodian's written permission
- ☐ Familial status protection also applies to pregnant women and anyone securing legal custody of a child under 18

Exemption: Housing for older persons is exempt from the prohibition against familial status discrimination if:

The HUD Secretary has determined that it is specifically designed for and occupied by:

- ☐ Elderly persons under a Federal, State or local government program
- ☐ It is occupied solely by persons who are 62 or older
- ☐ It houses at least one person who is 55 or older in at least 80 percent of the occupied units, and adheres to a policy that demonstrates an intent to house persons who are 55 or older
- ☐ A transition period permits residents on or before September 13, 1988, to continue living in the housing, regardless of their age, without interfering with the exemption

If You Think Your Rights Have Been Violated

HUD is ready to help with any problem of housing discrimination. If you think your rights have been violated, the Housing Discrimination Complaint Form is available for you to download, complete and return, or complete online and submit, or you may write HUD a letter, or telephone the HUD Office nearest you.

You have one year after an alleged violation to file a complaint with HUD, but you should file it as soon as possible.

What to Tell HUD:

- • Your name and address
- • The name and address of the person your complaint is against (the respondent)
- • The address or other identification to the housing involved
- • A short description to the alleged violation (the event that caused you to believe your rights were violated)

28

- The date(s) to the alleged violation

Where to Write or Call:

Send the Housing Discrimination Complaint Form or a letter to the HUD Office nearest you or you may call that office directly.

If You Are Disabled:

HUD also provides:

A toll-free TTY phone for the hearing-impaired: 1-800-927-9275.

- ✓ Interpreters
- ✓ Tapes and braille materials
- ✓ Assistance in reading and completing forms

What Happens when you file a complaint?

1. HUD will notify you when it receives your complaint

2. Notify the alleged violator of your complaint and permit that person to submit an answer

3. Investigate your complaint and determine whether there is reasonable cause to believe the Fair Housing Act has been violated

4. Notify you if it cannot complete an investigation within 100 days of receiving your complaint

5. Conciliation- HUD will try to reach an agreement with the person your complaint is against (the respondent)

   a. A conciliation agreement must protect both you and the public interest. If an agreement is signed, HUD will take no further action on your complaint.
   b. However, if HUD has reasonable cause to believe that a conciliation agreement is breached, HUD will recommend that the Attorney General file suit.

Complaint Referrals

If HUD has determined that your State or local agency has the same fair housing powers as HUD, HUD will refer your complaint to that agency for investigation and notify you of the referral. That agency must begin work on your complaint within 30 days or HUD may take it back.

What if You Need Help Quickly?

1. If you need immediate help to stop a serious problem that is being caused by a Fair Housing Act violation, HUD may be able to assist you as soon as you file a complaint. HUD may authorize the Attorney General to go to court to seek temporary or preliminary relief, pending the outcome of your complaint, if: Irreparable harm is likely to occur without HUD's intervention. There is substantial evidence that a violation of the Fair Housing Act occurred

Example: A builder agrees to sell a house but, after learning the buyer is black, fails to keep the agreement. The buyer files a complaint with HUD. HUD may authorize the Attorney General to go to court to prevent a sale to any other buyer until HUD investigates the complaint.

What Happens after a complaint investigation?

If, after investigating your complaint, HUD finds reasonable cause to believe that discrimination occurred, it will inform you. Your case will be heard in an administrative hearing within 120 days, unless you or the respondent want the case to be heard in Federal District Court. Either way, there is no cost to you.

The Administrative Hearing:

If your case goes to an administrative hearing HUD attorneys will litigate the case on your behalf. You may intervene in the case and be represented by your own attorney if you wish. An Administrative Law Judge (ALA) will consider evidence from you and the respondent. If the ALA decides that discrimination occurred, the respondent can be ordered:

1. To compensate you for actual damages, including humiliation, pain and suffering
2. To provide injunctive or other equitable relief, for example, to make the housing available to you
3. To pay the Federal Government a civil penalty to vindicate the public interest. The maximum penalties are $16,000 for a first violation and $65,000 for a third violation within seven years
4. To pay reasonable attorney's fees and costs
5. Federal District Court

If you or the respondent choose to have your case decided in Federal District Court, the Attorney General will file a suit and litigate it on your behalf. Like the ALA, the District Court can order relief, and award actual damages, attorney's fees and costs. In addition, the court can award punitive damages.

In Addition

You May File Suit: You may file suit, at your expense, in Federal District Court or State court within two years of an alleged violation. If you cannot afford an attorney, the court may appoint one for you. You may bring suit even after filing a complaint, if you have not signed a conciliation agreement and an Administrative Law Judge has not started a hearing. A court may award actual and punitive damages and attorney's fees and costs.

Other Tools to Combat Housing Discrimination:

If there is noncompliance with the order of an Administrative Law Judge, HUD may seek temporary relief, enforcement of the order or a restraining order in a United States Court of Appeals.

The Attorney General may file a suit in a Federal District Court if there is reasonable cause to believe a pattern or practice of housing discrimination is occurring.

For Further Information:

The Fair Housing Act and HUD's regulations contain more detail and technical information. If you need a copy of the law or regulations, contact the HUD Office nearest you.

Unsure? Questions? Let us know, we're here to help!

If You Live In The Following Areas/States:	Call The Toll-free Telephone Number	HUD Regional Office*
Connecticut, Maine, Massachusetts, New Hampshire, Rhode Island, Vermont	(800) 827-5005	**Boston**
New Jersey, New York, Puerto Rico, Virgin Islands	(800) 496-4294	**New York**
Delaware, District of Columbia, Maryland, Pennsylvania, Virginia, West Virginia	(888)799-2085	**Philadelphia**
	(800) 440-8091	**Atlanta**
Illinois, Indiana, Michigan, Minnesota, Ohio, Wisconsin	(800) 765-9372	**Chicago**
Arkansas, Louisiana, New Mexico, Oklahoma, Texas	(888) 560-8913	**Ft. Worth**
Iowa, Kansas, Missouri, Nebraska	(800) 743-5323	**Kansas City**
Colorado, Montana, North Dakota, South Dakota, Utah, Wyoming	(800) 877-7353	**Denver**
American Samoa, Arizona, California, Guam, Hawaii, Nevada	(800) 347-3739	**San Francisco**
Alaska, Idaho, Oregon, Washington	(800) 877-0246	**Seattle**

Your housing discrimination complaint will be reviewed by a fair housing specialist to determine if it alleges acts that might violate the Fair Housing Act. The specialist will assist you in filing an official housing discrimination complaint.

REAL ESTATE TERMS

1. **AMORTIZATION**—A method of paying for a loan by a series of regular payments. These payments reduce the principal and pay the cost of interest for the period on the unpaid balance

2. **APPRAISAL**—the process by which a value is placed on real estate or other property

3. **APPRECIATION**—the rise in value of property

4. **BALLOON PAYMENT**—a larger payment made at the end of a loan period that settles the balance of the amount borrowed

5. **BENEFICIARY**—A person who is named to receive a benefit, such as money or other value

6. **BUILDING CODES**—Community ordinances which regulate the structure of buildings

7. **CLEANING DEPOSIT**—A deposit to cover costs of cleaning an apartment

8. **CLEANING FEE**—a fee charged for cleaning an apartment. Usually not refunded

9. **CLOSING COSTS**—Charges such as building inspection, lot survey, prorated taxes, costs of an appraisal, Title Insurance, transfer taxes, and commissions

10. **COMMISSION**—A percentage of money earned by an agent as pay

11. **CONDOMINIUM**—Individual ownership of the unit you live in combined with joint ownership with others of common areas (halls, parking lot, etc.)

12. **CONTINGENCY**—some act or occurrence that depends upon certain conditions

13. **CONVEY**—the transfer or sale of real estate

14. **DEED**—a legal document that transfers title to real property

15. **DEFAULT**—Failure to do what one is obligated to do

16. **DEPOSIT RECEIPT**—A written statement given in return for a payment from a person offering to purchase property under certain conditions

17. DEPRECIATION—Decrease in value of property

18. DUPLEX—two single-family dwellings joined together

19. EARNEST MONEY—the deposit paid by a buyer to bind the contract

20. EASEMENT—a legal agreement that gives specified people the right to use another person's land for a certain purpose

21. EMINENT DOMAIN—The power of a government to purchase property at a fair price from an owner if it is needed for public use

22. EQUITY—an ownership interest . . . the difference between the present value of something and the amount still owed on it

23. ESCROW—Placing papers or money with a third party with the understanding that it will be delivered when certain conditions are met

24. ESCROW HOLDER—the person who holds the papers or money during an escrow transaction

25. EVICTION NOTICE—a legal notice that a tenant is subject to being removed from property by force, if necessary

26. FHA—Federal Housing Authority

27. FULLY AMORTIZED LOAN—each payment is for the same amount. A larger percentage of each payment applies to principal

28. HABITABLE—Livable conditions

29. HEIR—A person who receives an inheritance

30. INHERITANCE—Anything of value which may be acquired from ancestors

31. INTEREST—the amount paid for the use of money

32. LANDLORD—an owner of property who rents it to others

33. LEASE—a contract by which property is rented for a certain period of time

34. LESSEE—one who rents property under a lease contract

35. LENDING COMPANY—financial institutions that make loans on real estate

36. LESSOR—owner who leases to a tenant

37. LIEN—a money claim on property to make certain that a debt will be paid

38. MOBILE HOME—A complete living unit on wheels

39. MORTGAGEE—A person who gets a mortgage and who loans the money on property

40. MORTGAGE—A document that gives the right to the lending agency, under certain conditions, to reclaim property on which they have lent money

41. MORTGAGOR—the person who borrows money on property. The person who puts a mortgage on the property to secure the amount borrowed

42. MULTIPLE LISTING SERVICE—A system whereby description of property for sale are shared with other real estate agencies

43. ORAL RENTAL AGREEMENT—an unwritten rental agreement

44. OWNER—the person who has the title and rights to the property

45. PARTIALLY AMORTIZED LOAN—Principal is repaid in equal amounts and interest is paid only on the unpaid balance

46. PERMANENT FIXTURE—anything attached permanently to property and legally considered a part of it

47. PERSONAL PROPERTY—All movable property and anything not permanently attached to the land

48. PRINCIPAL—the person who is assisted by a broker in a real estate transaction

49. Also: A sum of money loaned, borrowed or invested

50. PROMISSORY NOTE—Primary evidence of debt with the obligation or promise secured by a Deed of Trust

51. PROPERTY—all things a person owns or may own

52. Your property includes all of your rights as well

53. (See Real Property and Personal Property)

54. PRORATION—Adjustment of interest, taxes and insurance, etc.

55. PURCHASE CONTRACT—a document whereby the owner agrees to sell and the buyer agrees to buy

56. REAL ESTATE—the land and all that is fixed to it

57. **REAL ESTATE BROKER**—A person who is responsible for the activities of the real estate firm and all of the associates associated with the firm

58. **REAL ESTATE SALES ASSOCIATE**—Any person employed or engaged by, or associated as an independent contractor with, or on behalf of, a real estate broker to do or deal in any act, acts or transactions set out in the definition of a real estate broker

59. **REAL PROPERTY**—the land and all that is fixed to it

60. **REALTIST**—A real estate broker who is a member of the National Association of Real Estate Brokers

61. **REALTOR**—A real estate broker who is a member of the National Association of Realtors

62. **RENT**—the amount paid for the use of property for a limited time

63. **ROW HOUSING**—a number of single-family dwellings jointed together

64. **SINGLE PARTY BROKER**—A person who works for the benefit of a party in a real estate transaction

65. **SUBLEASE**—an agreement whereby you lease or rent your apartment to someone else

66. **TENANT**—O ne who lives on property but does not own it

67. **TITLE**—the right of ownership

68. **TITLE INSURANCE**—insurance that assures the buyer and seller as to the title of the property. Title Company agrees to pay any claims not revealed to the extent of the policy

69. **TOWN HOUSE**—another name for two-story row housing

70. **TRANSACTION BROKER**—A person who assists a party and brings parties together and, for a fee or commission, assists them in conducting a real estate transaction. A transaction broker does not work for the benefit of the party

71. **TRIPLEX**—three single-family dwelling units jointed together

72. **UNAMORTIZED LOAN**—Payments are for interest only entire principal is repaid at the end of the loan period

73. **VA**—Veteran's Administration

74. WRITTEN RENTAL AGREEMENT—a rental contact that lists the terms and the amount of rent

75. ZONING—An act by a legal body which limits property use the limit is usually on use in a Specific area

Workbook
Budgeting, Credit, &
Housing

180 TRAINING.NET

Tell Us About Yourself

Print clearly. Use additional sheets if necessary.

Information will not be shared with any third party (e.g. credit agency or lender) without your explicit signed authorization.

General Information

Last Name:

First Name:

Middle Name:

Suffix (Sr., Jr., etc):

Social Security Number:

Home Phone:

Alternate Phone: Ext:

E-mail Address:

Birth Date:

Number of Dependents:

Gender: ☐ Female   ☐ Male

Marital Status: ☐ Married   ☐ Separated   ☐ Unmarried

☐ Single Head of Household

☐ Female Head of Household

☐ First Time Home Buyer

☐ US Veteran

☐ Owned Home in Last 3 Years

Race: ☐ American Indian/Alaskan Native

☐ Asian/Pacific Islander

☐ Black/Non-Hispanic

☐ Hispanic

☐ White/Non-Hispanic

☐ Other

Citizenship: ☐ US Citizen

☐ Permanent Resident

☐ Non-Resident

Address & Employment

Address ☐ Current

Street Address:

City: State: Zip:

Residency Status: ☐ Own   ☐ Rent

County:

Length of occupancy: Years: Months:

Previous Address (enter if the current address is less than 2 years)

Street Address:

City: State: Zip:

Residency Status: ☐ Own   ☐ Rent

County:

Length of occupancy: Years: Months:

Employment

Employer Name:

Street Address:

City: State: Zip:

Contact Phone: Ext:

Position/Title:

Start Date: End Date: ☐ Self Employed

Previous Employment (enter if within the last 2 years)

Employer Name:

Street Address:

City: State: Zip:

Contact Phone: Ext:

Position/Title:

Start Date: End Date: ☐ Self Employed

Financials

Income

Owner   If there are multiple clients, enter the name of the one responsible for the income
Type of Income   Specify the type of income: salary, commissions, bonuses, etc.
Pay Cycle   Indicate how frequently the client receives this income: biweekly, hourly, monthly, semi-monthly, weekly, or yearly

Owner: [　　　]　Type of Income: [　　　]　Amount: [　　　]　Pay Cycle: [　　　]

Owner: [　　　]　Type of Income: [　　　]　Amount: [　　　]　Pay Cycle: [　　　]

Owner: [　　　]　Type of Income: [　　　]　Amount: [　　　]　Pay Cycle: [　　　]

Owner: [　　　]　Type of Income: [　　　]　Amount: [　　　]　Pay Cycle: [　　　]

Owner: [　　　]　Type of Income: [　　　]　Amount: [　　　]　Pay Cycle: [　　　]

Assets

Owner   If there are multiple clients, enter the name of the one who owns the asset
Type of Asset   Describe the nature of the asset: checking account, savings account, stock, pending tax refund etc
Institution   Enter the name of the bank or other financial institution holding the asset

Owner   Type of Asset

Institution Name   Account Number   Asset Value   Available Funds

Owner   Type of Asset

Institution Name   Account Number   Asset Value   Available Funds

Owner   Type of Asset

Institution Name   Account Number   Asset Value   Available Funds

Owner   Type of Asset

Institution Name   Account Number   Asset Value   Available Funds

Owner   Type of Asset

Institution Name   Account Number   Asset Value   Available Funds

Financials (cont.)

Liabilities

Owner   If there are multiple clients, enter the name of the one who has the liability
Type of Liability   Describe the nature of the liability: credit line, mortgage, taxes, etc

Owner	Creditor Name	Account Number	Monthly Payment
	Type of Liability	Outstanding Balance	☐ Delinquent
Owner	Creditor Name	Account Number	Monthly Payment
	Type of Liability	Outstanding Balance	☐ Delinquent
Owner	Creditor Name	Account Number	Monthly Payment
	Type of Liability	Outstanding Balance	☐ Delinquent
Owner	Creditor Name	Account Number	Monthly Payment
	Type of Liability	Outstanding Balance	☐ Delinquent
Owner	Creditor Name	Account Number	Monthly Payment
	Type of Liability	Outstanding Balance	☐ Delinquent

Declarations (Credit Issues)

Owner   If there are multiple clients, enter the name of the one who had the issue
Action type   Specify one of the following: bankruptcy, foreclosure, judgement, lien, party to lawsuit, or repossession

Owner:	Action Type:	Date Occurred:	Resolution Date:
Owner:	Action Type:	Date Occurred:	Resolution Date:
Owner:	Action Type:	Date Occurred:	Resolution Date:

Non-Traditional Credit

Owner   If there are multiple clients, enter the name of the one responsible for this credit
Credit Type   Specify one of the following: auto insurance, cable TV, child care, electric, gas, homeowner/renter's insurance, life insurance, local merchant account, medical bill, medical insurance, rent, school tuition, telephone, or water

Owner:	Credit Type:	Average Monthly Payment:	☐ Doc. Provided
Owner:	Credit Type:	Average Monthly Payment:	☐ Doc. Provided
Owner:	Credit Type:	Average Monthly Payment:	☐ Doc. Provided
Owner:	Credit Type:	Average Monthly Payment:	☐ Doc. Provided
Owner:	Credit Type:	Average Monthly Payment:	☐ Doc. Provided

CREDIT REPORT AUTHORIZATION AND PRIVACY DISCLOSURE FORM

I hereby authorize and instruct _____ (hereinafter
"_____") to obtain and review my credit report. My credit report will be obtained from a credit reporting agency chosen by _____. I understand and agree that _____ intends to use the credit report for the purpose of evaluating my financial readiness to purchase a home and/or to engage in post-purchase counseling activities.

My signature below also authorizes the release to credit reporting agencies of financial or other information that I have supplied to _____ in connection with such evaluation. Authorization is further granted to the credit reporting agency to use a copy of this form to obtain any information the credit reporting agency deems necessary to complete my credit report.

In addition, in connection with determining my ability to obtain a loan, I

     _____   authorize

     _____   do not authorize

_____ to share with potential mortgage lenders and/or counseling agencies my credit report and any information that I have provided, including any computations and assessments that have been produced based upon such information. These lenders may contact me to discuss loans for which I may be eligible, and these counseling agencies may contact me to discuss counseling services.

I understand that I may revoke my consent to these disclosures by notifying _____ in writing.

_____
Client's Name (Print)

_____
Client's Name (Print)

_____
Client's Signature

_____
Client's Signature

_____
Social Security Number

_____
Social Security Number

_____
Date

_____
Date

Client Name(s):

Budget Name:

Income							
Budget Category	Week 1	Week 2	Week 3	Week 4	Monthly Actual Income	Monthly Budgeted Income	Difference
Total Weekly Income							

Expenses							
Budget Category	Week 1	Week 2	Week 3	Week 4	Monthly Actual Expenses	Monthly Budgeted Expenses	Difference
Total Weekly Expenses							

					Total Actual Amount	Total Budgeted Amount	
	Week 1	Week 2	Week 3	Week 4			Difference
Total Income:							
Total Expenses:							
Income - Expenses:							
Cumulative Savings							

Income / Expense Summary

Monthly Income Worksheet

Figure Your Monthly Income

Your weekly pay	$ _____ (take-home pay)	X 52 ÷ 12	$ _____ (monthly income)

or

Your twice-a-month pay	$ _____ (take-home pay)	X 2	$ _____ (monthly income)

Your Monthly Take-home Pay $ _____ .

Figure Other Household Members' Monthly Income

Weekly pay	$ _____ (take-home pay)	X 52 ÷ 12	$ _____ (monthly income)

or

Twice-a-month pay	$ _____ (take-home pay)	X 2	$ _____ (monthly income)

Other Household Members' Take-home Pay $ _____

Other Monthly Income

Second job $ _____

Regular overtime $ _____

Public assistance $ _____

Child support $ _____

Pension $ _____

Social Security $ _____

Other $ _____

Total Other Monthly Income $ _____

Total Net Monthly Income $ _____

Monthly Expenses Worksheet

Housing
Rent or mortgage	$ _____
Heating *(gas or oil)*	$ _____
Electricity	$ _____
Water or sewage	$ _____
Telephones *(landlines and cell phones)*	$ _____
Renters or homeowners insurance	$ _____
(if not included in mortgage)	
Trash service	$ _____
Home maintenance and furnishings	$ _____
Cleaning supplies	$ _____
Lawn service	$ _____

Transportation
Gas	$ _____
Car payment	$ _____
Car insurance	$ _____
Car inspection	$ _____
Car repairs and maintenance	$ _____
License plates and registration fees	$ _____
Public transportation or taxi	$ _____
Parking and tolls	$ _____

Food
Groceries	$ _____
School lunches	$ _____
Work-related *(lunches and snacks)*	$ _____

Insurance
Health	$ _____
(medical and dental, if not payroll-deducted)	
Life	$ _____
Disability	$ _____

Medical
Doctor	$ _____
Dentist	$ _____
Prescriptions	$ _____

Childcare
Childcare or babysitters	$ _____
Child support or alimony	$ _____

Clothing
Clothing	$ _____
Laundry and dry cleaning	$ _____

Donations
Religious or charity	$ _____

Education
Tuition	$ _____
Books, papers and supplies	$ _____
Newspapers and magazines	$ _____
Lessons *(sports, dance, music)*	$ _____

Gifts
Birthdays	$ _____
Major holidays	$ _____

Personal
Barber or beauty shop	$ _____
Toiletries	$ _____
Children's allowances	$ _____
Tobacco products	$ _____
Beer, wine or liquor	$ _____

Entertainment
Movies, sporting events, concerts, etc.	$ _____
Video rentals	$ _____
Internet service	$ _____
Cable/satellite TV	$ _____
Restaurants and take-out meals	$ _____
Gambling and lottery tickets	$ _____
Fitness or social clubs	$ _____
Vacations/trips	$ _____
Hobbies or crafts	$ _____

Miscellaneous
Checking account and money order fees	$ _____
Pet care and supplies	$ _____
Postage	$ _____
Pictures and photo processing	$ _____
"Mad" money	$ _____

Debts
Student loan	$ _____
Credit card *(monthly minimum)*	$ _____
Credit card *(monthly minimum)*	$ _____
Credit card *(monthly minimum)*	$ _____
Medical bills	$ _____
Personal loan	$ _____

Other
Other	$ _____
Other	$ _____
Other	$ _____

Total Regular Monthly Expenses $ _____

Monthly Discretionary Income Worksheet

Figure Your Discretionary Income	Extra Money Each Month
Total Monthly Income	$ _____
Minus total regular monthly expenses	$ _____
Discretionary income *(Balance available to spend or save)*	$ _____

KEEPING TRACK OF YOUR SPENDING

The best way to find out where your money really goes is to begin keeping track of everything you and members of your household spend money on – from picking up the dry cleaning to getting shaving cream and greeting cards at the drug store to stopping for fast food to filling up at the gas station. Find a simple method of tracking that works for you, whether it be saving all receipts from purchases or giving each person a small notebook to write down expenditures.

The first step in taking command of your finances is to figure out where all the money is going. Only then can you redirect it for your benefit.

Look at your expenses weekly, and you may be surprised where the money goes. When you begin to develop a spending plan that includes saving for your goals, you can use your records to help you find places to cut your spending.

Monthly Spending Plan

This spending plan is broken down into the following types of expenses: fixed, periodic fixed, flexible and indebtedness. Depending on your situation, some expenses (for example, a cell phone) may be considered flexible rather than fixed. Be sure to adjust the categories to best reflect your needs and lifestyle.

	Monthly Expense	Budgeted Amount	Actual Spent	Difference
Fixed Expenses				
Housing	Rent or Mortgage			
	Heating (gas or oil)			
	Electricity			
	Telephones (landlines and cell phones)			
	Other:			
Transportation	Gas			
	Car Payment			
	Public Transportation or Taxi			
	Parking and Tolls			
	Other:			
Insurance	Health (medical and dental, if not payroll deducted)			
	Life			
	Disability			
	Other:			
Childcare	Childcare or Babysitters			
	Child Support or Alimony			
	Fixed Expenses Subtotal			
Periodic Fixed Expenses (divide annual payments by 12)				
Housing	Renters or Homeowners Insurance (if not included in mortgage)			
	Water or Sewage			
	Trash Service			
	Other:			
Transportation	Car Insurance			
	Car Inspection			
	Car Repairs and Maintenance			
	License Plates and Registration Fees			
	Other:			
	Periodic Fixed Expenses Subtotal			

	Monthly Expense	Budgeted Amount	Actual Spent	Difference
Flexible Expenses				
Food	Groceries			
	School Lunches			
	Work-Related (lunches and snacks)			
	Other:			
Housing	Home Maintenance and Furnishings			
	Cleaning Supplies			
	Lawn Care			
	Other:			
Medical	Doctor			
	Dentist			
	Prescriptions			
	Other:			
Savings	Emergency Fund			
	Down Payment Fund			
Clothing	Clothing			
	Laundry and Dry Cleaning			
	Other:			
Education	Tuition			
	Books, Papers and Supplies			
	Newspapers and Magazines			
	Lessons (sports, dance, music)			
	Other:			
Donations	Religious or Charity			
	Other (if not payroll deducted):			
Gifts	Birthdays			
	Holidays			
	Other:			
Personal	Barber or Beauty Shop			
	Toiletries			
	Children's Allowances			
	Tobacco Products			
	Beer, Wine, Liquor			
	Other:			

Source: CreditSmart by Freddie Mac

	Monthly Expense	Budgeted Amount	Actual Spent	Difference
Flexible Expenses Continued				
Entertainment	Movies, Sporting Events, Concerts, Theater, Etc.			
	Video Rentals			
	Internet Service			
	Cable/Satellite TV			
	Restaurants and Take-Out Meals			
	Gambling or Lottery Tickets			
	Fitness or Social Clubs			
	Vacations/Trips			
	Hobbies or Crafts			
	Other:			
Miscellaneous	Checking Account Fees, Money Order Fees, Etc.			
	Pet Care or Supplies			
	Postage			
	Pictures and Photo Processing			
	"Mad" Money			
	Other:			
	Flexible Expenses Subtotal			
Indebtedness Expenses				
Debt*	Student Loan			
	Credit Card (monthly minimum*)			
	Credit Card (monthly minimum)			
	Credit Card (monthly minimum)			
	Medical Bills			
	Personal Loan			
	Other:			
	Indebtedness Subtotal			
Total				
Total Monthly Expenses (fixed + periodic fixed + flexible + indebtedness)				
Income				
Total Monthly Net Income				
Additional Savings				
Amount Left Over for Savings (total monthly net income – total monthly expenses)				

*Although it is strongly recommended that you pay more than one monthly minimum payment due, lenders will use this amount when calculating monthly debt obligations.

The Basics

1. What part of town (or country) do you want to live in? _____

2. What price range would you consider? No less than _____ but no more than _____

3. Are schools a factor and, if so, what do you need to take into consideration (e.g., want specific school system, want kids to be able to walk to school, etc.)?
    _____

4. Do you want an older home or a newer home (less than 5 years old)? _____

5. What kind of houses would you be willing to see?

    _____One story _____2 story _____split foyer _____bi-level _____tri-level
    _____townhouse or condo _____mobile home

6. What style house appeals to you most?

    ____contemporary ____traditional ____southwestern ____colonial ____no preference

7. How much renovation would you be willing to do? A lot ____ A little ____ None! ____

8. Do you have to be close to public transportation?   _____yes _____no

9. Do you have any physical needs that must be met, such as wheelchair access? ____yes
    ____no

10. Do you have any animals that will require special facilities? _____yes _____no

         If so, what? _____

11. The Lot

	Must Have	Would Like to Have
Large yard (1 acre or more)	_____	_____
Small yard (less than 1 acre)	_____	_____
Fenced yard	_____	_____
Garage	_____	_____
Carport	_____	_____
Patio/deck	_____	_____
Pool	_____	_____
Outdoor spa	_____	_____
Extra parking	_____	_____
Other buildings (barn, shed, etc.)	_____	_____
Special view	_____	_____ Of what? _____

The Interior

12. How many bedrooms *must* you have? _____ would you like to have? _____

13. How many bathrooms do you want? _____

14. How big would you like your house to be (square feet)? No less than _____
But no more than _____

15. What features do you want to have in your house?

	Must have	Would Like to Have
Air conditioning	_____	_____
Wall-to-wall carpet	_____	_____
Ceramic tile	_____	_____
Hardwood floors	_____	_____
Eat-in kitchen	_____	_____
Separate dining room	_____	_____
Formal living room	_____	_____
Family room	_____	_____
Greatroom	_____	_____
Separate den or library	_____	_____
Basement	_____	_____
Separate laundry room	_____	_____
Fireplace	_____	_____
Workshop	_____	_____
No interior steps	_____	_____
"In-law" apartment	_____	_____
Spa in bathroom	_____	_____
Lots of windows (light)	_____	_____

Community features

16. Do you want to live in an area with a Community Association? _____yes _____no

17. What else do you want in your community?

	Must have	Would like to have
Community pool	_____	_____
Golf course	_____	_____
Basketball court	_____	_____
Tennis courts	_____	_____
Gated community or doorman	_____	_____
Clubhouse/activities	_____	_____

18. Are there any other special features or needs that you must consider when you're looking for a home?

MLS #00000005 - Active
Single Family

22100 Main Street	List Price: **$100,500**
Anytown, USA 00000	
Some County	

Total Rooms: 7   Bedrooms: **3**
Full/Half/Master Baths: **1/1/**   Fireplaces: 1
Unit Placement: --   Unit Level: **2**
Grade School: Middle School:
High School:
Directions: **Corner of Main and Elm Streets**

...marks

...acious family room w/10 ft ceiling. Operational fireplace. Large, spacious kitchen, 2 guest bedrooms, guest bath.
...rge bay window in front. Dining room features wainscoting. Fenced in yard.

...operty Information

...prox. Acres: **0**   Approx. Gross Living Area: **1422 sq. ft.** Garage Spaces: **0** --
...at Zones: 2 **Central Heat, Forced Air,**   Gross Living Area Source: **Other**   Parking Spaces: O**n Street**
...ol Zones: 2 **Central Air, Individual**   Living Levels: **2**

...omplex & Association Information

...mplex Name: Units in Complex: 0 Complete: N/A   Units Owner Occupied: 1 Source:
...sociation: **Yes** Fee: **$300**   Fee Includes: **Water, Sewer, Master Insurance, Exterior Maintenance**

...om Levels, Dimensions and Features

...om	Level	Size	Features
...ing Room:	2	12x14	**Fireplace, Hard Wood Floor**
...ing Room:	2	10x11	**Cathedral Ceiling, Hard Wood Floor**
...chen:	1	10x12	**Hard Wood Floor, Solid Counters**
...ster Bedroom:	1	13x15	**Hard Wood Floor**
...droom 2:	2	10x12	**Hard Wood Floor**
...droom 3:	2	9x11	**Hard Wood Floor**
...th 1:	1	10x10	**Hard Wood Floor, Solid Counters**
...her:	1	7x10	--

...atures

...ea Amenities: **Public Transportation, Swimming Pool, Park**
...pliances: **Wall Oven, Dishwasher, Disposal, Microwave, Countertop Range, Refrigerator, Freezer,**
...asher, Dryer
...sociation Pool: **No**
...sement: **Yes**
...ach: **No**
...nstruction: **Brick**
...cs in Hand: **Master Deed, Rules & Regs**
...ctric Features: **110 Volts, 220 Volts**
...ergy Features: **Insulated Windows, Prog. Thermostat**
...terior: **Brick**
...terior Features: **Deck, Enclosed Patio, Balcony, Storage Shed**
...ooring: **Wood**
...t Water: **Natural Gas**
...sulation Features: **Full**
...terior Features: **Security System, Cable Available**
...of Material: **Asphalt/Fiberglass Shingles**
...wer and Water: **City/Town Water, City/Town Sewer**
...lity Connections: **for Gas Range, for Electric Oven, for Electric Dryer, Washer Hookup, Icemaker**
...nnection
...aterfront: **No**

Other Property Info

Adult Community: **No**
Disclosure Declaration: **No**
Disclosures:
Exclusions:
Lead Paint: **None, Unknown**
UFFI: **Unknown** Warranty Available: **No**
Year Built/Converted: **1975**
Year Built Source: **Public Record**
Year Built Desc: **Actual**
Year Round: **Yes**

Tax Information

Pin #: **W:03 P:024591 S:003**
Assessed: **$99,400**
Tax: **$1657** Tax Year: **2006**
Book: **3341** Page: **301**
Cert:
Zoning Code: **RES**
Map: Block: Lot:

You'll want to make several copies of this checklist and fill one out for each home you tour. Then, comparing your ratings later will be easy.

THE HOME	Good	Average	Poor
Square footage			
Number of bedrooms			
Number of baths			
Practicality of floorplan			
Interior walls condition			
Closet/storage space			
Basement			
Fireplace			
Cable TV			
Basement: dampness or odors			
Exterior appearance, condition			
Lawn/yard space			
Fence			
Patio or deck			
Garage			
Energy efficiency			
Screens, storm windows			
Roof: age and condition			
Gutters and downspouts			

THE NEIGHBORHOOD	Good	Average	Poor
Appearance/condition of nearby homes/businesses			
Traffic			
Noise Level			
Safety/Security			
Age mix of inhabitants			
Number of children			
Pet restrictions			

THE NEIGHBORHOOD (Cont.)	Good	Average	Poor
Parking			
Zoning regulations			
Neighborhood restrictions/ covenants			
Fire protection			
Police			
Snow removal			
Garbage service			

SCHOOLS	Good	Average	Poor
Age/condition			
Reputation			
Quality of teachers			
Achievement test scores			
Play areas			
Curriculum			
Class size			
Busing distance			

CONVENIENCE TO:	Good	Average	Poor
Supermarket			
Schools			
Work			
Shopping			
Child care			
Hospitals			
Doctor/dentist			
Recreation/parks			
Restaurants/entertainment			
Church/synagogue			
Airport			
Highways			
Public transportation			

Good Faith Estimate (GFE)

Name of Originator		Borrower	
Originator Address		Property Address	
Originator Phone Number			
Originator Email		Date of GFE	

Purpose

This GFE gives you an estimate of your settlement charges and loan terms if you are approved for this loan. For more information, see HUD's *Special Information Booklet* on settlement charges, your *Truth-in-Lending Disclosures*, and other consumer information at www.hud.gov/respa. If you decide you would like to proceed with this loan, contact us.

Shopping for your loan

Only you can shop for the best loan for you. Compare this GFE with other loan offers, so you can find the best loan. Use the shopping chart on page 3 to compare all the offers you receive.

Important dates

1. The interest rate for this GFE is available through [_____]. After this time, the interest rate, some of your loan Origination Charges, and the monthly payment shown below can change until you lock your interest rate.

2. This estimate for all other settlement charges is available through [_____].

3. After you lock your interest rate, you must go to settlement within [___] days (your rate lock period) to receive the locked interest rate.

4. You must lock the interest rate at least [___] days before settlement.

Summary of your loan

Your initial loan amount is	$
Your loan term is	years
Your initial interest rate is	%
Your initial monthly amount owed for principal, interest, and any mortgage insurance is	$ per month
Can your interest rate rise?	☐ No ☐ Yes, it can rise to a maximum of %. The first change will be in .
Even if you make payments on time, can your loan balance rise?	☐ No ☐ Yes, it can rise to a maximum of $
Even if you make payments on time, can your monthly amount owed for principal, interest, and any mortgage insurance rise?	☐ No ☐ Yes, the first increase can be in and the monthly amount owed can rise to $. The maximum it can ever rise to is $.
Does your loan have a prepayment penalty?	☐ No ☐ Yes, your maximum prepayment penalty is $.
Does your loan have a balloon payment?	☐ No ☐ Yes, you have a balloon payment of $ due in years.

Escrow account information

Some lenders require an escrow account to hold funds for paying property taxes or other property-related charges in addition to your monthly amount owed of $[_____].
Do we require you to have an escrow account for your loan?
☐ No, you do not have an escrow account. You must pay these charges directly when due.
☐ Yes, you have an escrow account. It may or may not cover all of these charges. Ask us.

Summary of your settlement charges

A	Your Adjusted Origination Charges *(See page 2.)*	$
B	Your Charges for All Other Settlement Services *(See page 2.)*	$
A + B	Total Estimated Settlement Charges	$

Understanding your estimated settlement charges

Some of these charges can change at settlement. See the top of page 3 for more information.

Your Adjusted Origination Charges

1. Our origination charge
This charge is for getting this loan for you.

2. Your credit or charge (points) for the specific interest rate chosen

☐ The credit or charge for the interest rate of ☐ % is included in "Our origination charge." (See item 1 above.)

☐ You receive a credit of $ ☐ for this interest rate of ☐ %. This credit **reduces** your settlement charges.

☐ You pay a charge of $ ☐ for this interest rate of ☐ %. This charge (points) **increases** your total settlement charges.

The tradeoff table on page 3 shows that you can change your total settlement charges by choosing a different interest rate for this loan.

A	Your Adjusted Origination Charges	$

Your Charges for All Other Settlement Services

3. Required services that we select
These charges are for services we require to complete your settlement. We will choose the providers of these services.

Service	Charge

4. Title services and lender's title insurance
This charge includes the services of a title or settlement agent, for example, and title insurance to protect the lender, if required.

5. Owner's title insurance
You may purchase an owner's title insurance policy to protect your interest in the property.

6. Required services that you can shop for
These charges are for other services that are required to complete your settlement. We can identify providers of these services or you can shop for them yourself. Our estimates for providing these services are below.

Service	Charge

7. Government recording charges
These charges are for state and local fees to record your loan and title documents.

8. Transfer taxes
These charges are for state and local fees on mortgages and home sales.

9. Initial deposit for your escrow account
This charge is held in an escrow account to pay future recurring charges on your property and includes ☐ all property taxes, ☐ all insurance, and ☐ other ☐ .

10. Daily interest charges
This charge is for the daily interest on your loan from the day of your settlement until the first day of the next month or the first day of your normal mortgage payment cycle. This amount is $ ☐ per day for ☐ days (if your settlement is ☐).

11. Homeowner's insurance
This charge is for the insurance you must buy for the property to protect from a loss, such as fire.

Policy	Charge

B	Your Charges for All Other Settlement Services	$

A + B	Total Estimated Settlement Charges	$

Instructions

Understanding which charges can change at settlement

This GFE estimates your settlement charges. At your settlement, you will receive a HUD-1, a form that lists your actual costs. Compare the charges on the HUD-1 with the charges on this GFE. Charges can change if you select your own provider and do not use the companies we identify. (See below for details.)

These charges cannot increase at settlement:	The total of these charges can increase up to 10% at settlement:	These charges can change at settlement:
■ Our origination charge ■ Your credit or charge (points) for the specific interest rate chosen (after you lock in your interest rate) ■ Your adjusted origination charges (after you lock in your interest rate) ■ Transfer taxes	■ Required services that we select ■ Title services and lender's title insurance (if we select them or you use companies we identify) ■ Owner's title insurance (if you use companies we identify) ■ Required services that you can shop for (if you use companies we identify) ■ Government recording charges	■ Required services that you can shop for (if you do not use companies we identify) ■ Title services and lender's title insurance (if you do not use companies we identify) ■ Owner's title insurance (if you do not use companies we identify) ■ Initial deposit for your escrow account ■ Daily interest charges ■ Homeowner's insurance

Using the tradeoff table

In this GFE, we offered you this loan with a particular interest rate and estimated settlement charges. However:
- If you want to choose this same loan with **lower settlement charges,** then you will have a **higher interest rate.**
- If you want to choose this same loan with a **lower interest rate,** then you will have **higher settlement charges.**

If you would like to choose an available option, you must ask us for a new GFE.

Loan originators have the option to complete this table. Please ask for additional information if the table is not completed.

	The loan in this GFE	The same loan with lower settlement charges	The same loan with a lower interest rate
Your initial loan amount	$	$	$
Your initial interest rate¹	%	%	%
Your initial monthly amount owed	$	$	$
Change in the monthly amount owed from this GFE	No change	You will pay $ **more** every month	You will pay $ **less** every month
Change in the amount you will pay at settlement with this interest rate	No change	Your settlement charges will be **reduced** by $	Your settlement charges will **increase** by $
How much your total estimated settlement charges will be	$	$	$

¹ *For an adjustable rate loan, the comparisons above are for the initial interest rate before adjustments are made.*

Using the shopping chart

Use this chart to compare GFEs from different loan originators. Fill in the information by using a different column for each GFE you receive. By comparing loan offers, you can shop for the best loan.

	This loan	Loan 2	Loan 3	Loan 4
Loan originator name				
Initial loan amount				
Loan term				
Initial interest rate				
Initial monthly amount owed				
Rate lock period				
Can interest rate rise?				
Can loan balance rise?				
Can monthly amount owed rise?				
Prepayment penalty?				
Balloon payment?				
Total Estimated Settlement Charges				

If your loan is sold in the future

Some lenders may sell your loan after settlement. Any fees lenders receive in the future cannot change the loan you receive or the charges you paid at settlement.

REAL ESTATE AGENCY DISCLOSURE
AND ELECTION (This is NOT an employment agreement.)

THE PRINTED PORTION OF THIS FORM HAS BEEN APPROVED BY THE ARIZONA ASSOCIATION OF REALTORS®. NO REPRESENTATION IS MADE AS TO THE LEGAL VALIDITY OR ADEQUACY OF ANY PROVISION OR THE TAX CONSEQUENCES THEREOF. IF YOU DESIRE LEGAL OR TAX ADVICE, CONSULT YOUR ATTORNEY.

1. FIRM NAME ("BROKER")_____

2. acting through _____ hereby makes the following disclosure.
   (LICENSEE'S NAME)

DISCLOSURE

3. Before a Seller/Landlord ("Seller") or a Buyer/Tenant ("Buyer") enters into a discussion with a real estate broker or licensee affiliated
4. with a broker, the Seller and the Buyer should understand what type of agency relationship or representation they will have with the
5. broker in the transaction.

6. **I. Buyer's Broker:** A broker other than the Seller's broker can agree with the Buyer to act as the broker for the Buyer. In these
7. situations, the Buyer's broker is not representing the Seller, even if the Buyer's broker is receiving compensation for services
8. rendered, either in full or in part, from the Seller or through the Seller's broker:
9. a) A Buyer's broker has the fiduciary duties of loyalty, obedience, disclosure, confidentiality, and accounting in dealings with the Buyer.
10. b) Other potential Buyers represented by broker may consider, make offers on, or acquire an interest in the same or similar properties
11. as Buyer is seeking.

12. **II. Seller's Broker:** A broker under a listing agreement with the Seller acts as the broker for the Seller only:
13. a) A Seller's broker has the fiduciary duties of loyalty, obedience, disclosure, confidentiality, and accounting in dealings with the Seller.
14. b) Other potential Sellers represented by broker may list properties that are similar to the property that Seller is selling.

15. **III. Broker Representing both Seller and Buyer (Limited Representation):** A broker, either acting directly or through one or more
16. licensees within the same brokerage firm, can legally represent both the Seller and the Buyer in a transaction, but only with the
17. knowledge and informed consent of both the Seller and the Buyer. In these situations, the Broker, acting through its licensee(s),
18. represents both the Buyer and the Seller, with limitations of the duties owed to the Buyer and the Seller:
19. a) The broker will not, without written authorization, disclose to the other party that the Seller will accept a price or terms other
20. than stated in the listing or that the Buyer will accept a price or terms other than offered.
21. b) There will be conflicts in the duties of loyalty, obedience, disclosure and confidentiality. Disclosure of confidential information
22. may be made only with written authorization.

23. Regardless of who the Broker represents in the transaction, the Broker shall exercise reasonable skill and care in the performance of
24. the Broker's duties and shall be truthful and honest to both the Buyer and Seller and shall disclose all known facts which materially and
25. adversely affect the consideration to be paid by any party. Pursuant to A.R.S. §32-2156, Sellers, Lessors and Brokers are not obligated
26. to disclose that a property is or has been: (1) the site of a natural death, suicide, homicide, or any crime classified as a felony; (2)
27. owned or occupied by a person exposed to HIV, or diagnosed as having AIDS or any other disease not known to be transmitted
28. through common occupancy of real estate; or (3) located in the vicinity of a sex offender. Sellers or Sellers' representatives may not
29. treat the existence, terms, or conditons of offers as confidential unless there is a confidentiality agreement between the parties.

30. **THE DUTIES OF THE BROKER IN A REAL ESTATE TRANSACTION DO NOT RELIEVE THE SELLER OR THE BUYER FROM THE**
31. **RESPONSIBILITY TO PROTECT THEIR OWN INTERESTS. THE SELLER AND THE BUYER SHOULD CAREFULLY READ ALL**
32. **AGREEMENTS TO INSURE THAT THE DOCUMENTS ADEQUATELY EXPRESS THEIR UNDERSTANDING OF THE TRANSACTION.**

ELECTION

33. **Buyer Election** (Complete this section only if you are the Buyer.)
34. The undersigned elects to have the Broker (check any that apply):
35. ☐ represent the Buyer as Buyer's Broker.
36. ☐ represent the Seller as Seller's Broker.
37. ☐ show Buyer properties listed with Broker's firm and Buyer agrees that Broker shall act as agent for both Buyer and Seller
38. provided that the Seller consents to limited representation. In the event of a purchase, Buyer's and Seller's informed consent should be
39. acknowledged in a separate writing other than the purchase contract.

40. **Seller Election** (Complete this section only if you are the Seller.)
41. The undersigned elects to have the Broker (check any that apply):
42. ☐ represent the Buyer as Buyer's Broker.
43. ☐ represent the Seller as Seller's Broker.
44. ☐ show Seller's property to Buyers represented by Broker's firm and Seller agrees that Broker shall act as agent for both Buyer and Seller
45. provided that Buyer consents to the limited representation. In the event of a purchase, Buyer's and Seller's informed consent should be
46. acknowledged in a separate writing other than the purchase contract.

47. The undersigned ☐ Buyer(s) or ☐ Seller(s) acknowledge that this document is a disclosure of duties. This document is not an
48. employment agreement.

49. I/ WE ACKNOWLEDGE RECEIPT OF A COPY OF THIS DISCLOSURE.

50. **SAMPLE** _____   **SAMPLE** _____
    PRINT NAME   PRINT NAME

51. **SAMPLE** _____   **SAMPLE** _____
    SIGNED   MO/DA/YR   SIGNED   MO/DA/YR

This form is available for use by the entire real estate industry. The use of this form is not intended to identify the user as a REALTOR®. REALTOR® is a registered collective membership mark that may be used only by real estate licensees who are members of the NATIONAL ASSOCIATION OF REALTORS® and who subscribe to its Code of Ethics.
®ARIZONA ASSOCIATION OF REALTORS® FORM 1587-1555 READAE 1/06

OMB Approval No. 2502-0265

A. **Settlement Statement (HUD-1)**

B. Type of Loan		

1. ☐ FHA 2. ☐ RHS 3. ☐ Conv. Unins.	6. File Number:	7. Loan Number:	8. Mortgage Insurance Case Number:
4. ☐ VA 5. ☐ Conv. Ins.			

C. Note: This form is furnished to give you a statement of actual settlement costs. Amounts paid to and by the settlement agent are shown. Items marked "(p.o.c.)" were paid outside the closing; they are shown here for informational purposes and are not included in the totals.

D. Name & Address of Borrower:	E. Name & Address of Seller:	F. Name & Address of Lender:
G. Property Location:	H. Settlement Agent:	I. Settlement Date:
	Place of Settlement:	

J. Summary of Borrower's Transaction		**K. Summary of Seller's Transaction**	
100. Gross Amount Due from Borrower		**400. Gross Amount Due to Seller**	
101. Contract sales price		401. Contract sales price	
102. Personal property		402. Personal property	
103. Settlement charges to borrower (line 1400)		403.	
104.		404.	
105.		405.	
Adjustment for items paid by seller in advance		**Adjustment for items paid by seller in advance**	
106. City/town taxes to		406. City/town taxes to	
107. County taxes to		407. County taxes to	
108. Assessments to		408. Assessments to	
109.		409.	
110.		410.	
111.		411.	
112.		412.	
120. Gross Amount Due from Borrower		**420. Gross Amount Due to Seller**	
200. Amount Paid by or in Behalf of Borrower		**500. Reductions In Amount Due to seller**	
201. Deposit or earnest money		501. Excess deposit (see instructions)	
202. Principal amount of new loan(s)		502. Settlement charges to seller (line 1400)	
203. Existing loan(s) taken subject to		503. Existing loan(s) taken subject to	
204.		504. Payoff of first mortgage loan	
205.		505. Payoff of second mortgage loan	
206.		506.	
207.		507.	
208.		508.	
209.		509.	
Adjustments for items unpaid by seller		**Adjustments for items unpaid by seller**	
210. City/town taxes to		510. City/town taxes to	
211. County taxes to		511. County taxes to	
212. Assessments to		512. Assessments to	
213.		513.	
214.		514.	
215.		515.	
216.		516.	
217.		517.	
218.		518.	
219.		519.	
220. Total Paid by/for Borrower		**520. Total Reduction Amount Due Seller**	
300. Cash at Settlement from/to Borrower		**600. Cash at Settlement to/from Seller**	
301. Gross amount due from borrower (line 120)		601. Gross amount due to seller (line 420)	
302. Less amounts paid by/for borrower (line 220)	( )	602. Less reductions in amounts due seller (line 520)	( )
303. Cash ☐ From ☐ To Borrower		603. Cash ☐ To ☐ From Seller	

The Public Reporting Burden for this collection of information is estimated at 35 minutes per response for collecting, reviewing, and reporting the data. This agency may not collect this information, and you are not required to complete this form, unless it displays a currently valid OMB control number. No confidentiality is assured; this disclosure is mandatory. This is designed to provide the parties to a RESPA covered transaction with information during the settlement process.

L. Settlement Charges

	Paid From Borrower's Funds at Settlement	Paid From Seller's Funds at Settlement
700. Total Real Estate Broker Fees		
Division of commission (line 700) as follows :		
701. $ to		
702. $ to		
703. Commission paid at settlement		
704.		

800. Items Payable in Connection with Loan		
801. Our origination charge $ (from GFE #1)		
802. Your credit or charge (points) for the specific interest rate chosen $ (from GFE #2)		
803. Your adjusted origination charges (from GFE #A)		
804. Appraisal fee to (from GFE #3)		
805. Credit report to (from GFE #3)		
806. Tax service to (from GFE #3)		
807. Flood certification to (from GFE #3)		
808.		
809.		
810.		
811.		

900. Items Required by Lender to be Paid in Advance		
901. Daily interest charges from to @ $ /day (from GFE #10)		
902. Mortgage insurance premium for months to (from GFE #3)		
903. Homeowner's insurance for years to (from GFE #11)		
904.		

1000. Reserves Deposited with Lender		
1001. Initial deposit for your escrow account (from GFE #9)		
1002. Homeowner's insurance months @ $ per month $		
1003. Mortgage insurance months @ $ per month $		
1004. Property Taxes months @ $ per month $		
1005. months @ $ per month $		
1006. months @ $ per month $		
1007. Aggregate Adjustment -$		

1100. Title Charges		
1101. Title services and lender's title insurance (from GFE #4)		
1102. Settlement or closing fee $		
1103. Owner's title insurance (from GFE #5)		
1104. Lender's title insurance $		
1105. Lender's title policy limit $		
1106. Owner's title policy limit $		
1107. Agent's portion of the total title insurance premium to $		
1108. Underwriter's portion of the total title insurance premium to $		
1109.		
1110.		
1111.		

1200. Government Recording and Transfer Charges		
1201. Government recording charges (from GFE #7)		
1202. Deed $ Mortgage $ Release $		
1203. Transfer taxes (from GFE #8)		
1204. City/County tax/stamps Deed $ Mortgage $		
1205. State tax/stamps Deed $ Mortgage $		
1206.		

1300. Additional Settlement Charges		
1301. Required services that you can shop for (from GFE #6)		
1302. $		
1303. $		
1304.		
1305.		

1400. Total Settlement Charges (enter on lines 103, Section J and 502, Section K)		

Comparison of Good Faith Estimate (GFE) and HUD-1 Charrges		Good Faith Estimate	HUD-1
Charges That Cannot Increase	HUD-1 Line Number		
Our origination charge	# 801		
Your credit or charge (points) for the specific interest rate chosen	# 802		
Your adjusted origination charges	# 803		
Transfer taxes	# 1203		

Charges That In Total Cannot Increase More Than 10%		Good Faith Estimate	HUD-1
Government recording charges	# 1201		
	#		
	#		
	#		
	#		
	#		
	#		
	#		
Total			
Increase between GFE and HUD-1 Charges		$ or %	

Charges That Can Change			Good Faith Estimate	HUD-1
Initial deposit for your escrow account		# 1001		
Daily interest charges	$ /day	# 901		
Homeowner's insurance		# 903		
		#		
		#		
		#		

Loan Terms

Your initial loan amount is	$
Your loan term is	years
Your initial interest rate is	%
Your initial monthly amount owed for principal, interest, and any mortgage insurance is	$ includes ☐ Principal ☐ Interest ☐ Mortgage Insurance
Can your interest rate rise?	☐ No ☐ Yes, it can rise to a maximum of %. The first change will be on and can change again every after . Every change date, your interest rate can increase or decrease by %. Over the life of the loan, your interest rate is guaranteed to never be lower than % or higher than %.
Even if you make payments on time, can your loan balance rise?	☐ No ☐ Yes, it can rise to a maximum of $
Even if you make payments on time, can your monthly amount owed for principal, interest, and mortgage insurance rise?	☐ No ☐ Yes, the first increase can be on and the monthly amount owed can rise to $. The maximum it can ever rise to is $
Does your loan have a prepayment penalty?	☐ No ☐ Yes, your maximum prepayment penalty is $
Does your loan have a balloon payment?	☐ No ☐ Yes, you have a balloon payment of $ due in years on
Total monthly amount owed including escrow account payments	☐ You do not have a monthly escrow payment for items, such as property taxes and homeowner's insurance. You must pay these items directly yourself. ☐ You have an additional monthly escrow payment of $ that results in a total initial monthly amount owed of $. This includes principal, interest, any mortgage insurance and any items checked below: ☐ Property taxes ☐ Homeowner's insurance ☐ Flood insurance ☐ ☐ ☐

Note: If you have any questions about the Settlement Charges and Loan Terms listed on this form, please contact your lender.

Sample Homeowners Insurance Quote Form

Personal Information:

1st Named Insured	Date of Birth:	SSN:
Home Phone:	Cell Phone:	Email:
2nd Named Insured:	Date of Birth:	SSN:
Home Phone:	Cell Phone:	Email:
Mailing Address:	Township:	County:
	City/State	Zip Code:

Current Insurance Information:

Current Deductible:	Liability Limit: -- Choose a Liability Limi
Current Insurance Carrier:	Current Dwelling Amount:
Policy Start Date	Known Losses (past 5 years):

Home & Property Information:

Physical Address: Year Constructed: # Living in Home: # of Families:

Miles from Fire Dept.   Responding Fire Dept.

Fire Hydrant Near: Inside City Limits?   ○ Yes   ○ N

Wood Stove: ○ Yes ○ No   Fireplace: - Fireplace -   Age of Roof (Years):   Roof Type:

Above Ground Sq. Footage: House Style: - House Type -   % of Basement Finished:

Walkout Basement: ○ Yes ○ No   Age of Plumbing (Years):   # Full Bath: # ¾ Bath: # ½ Bath:

Heat Source & Type: Age of Heat Source (Years):   A/C Central Air: ○ Yes ○

Age of Electrical (Years):   Kitchen Type: - Kitchen Type -   Specialized Doors:

Other Special Features: Business Usage: ○ Yes ○ No

Garage: - Garage Type -   Garage Size: - Garage Size -

Attached Structures: Size of Structure: Security System: ○ Yes ○ N

Attached Structures: Size of Structure: Total Acreage:

Other Attached Structures: Size of Structure: Trampoline:

Swimming Pool: ○ Yes ○ No   Pool Type: - Pool Type -   Pool Extras: - Pool Extras

Pets *(list breed)*

Outbuildings?
If yes, please enter type, size, and value for each:

High Value Items?
Please enter all details for any Collectibles, Art, Jewelry, Guns, ATVs, Snowmobiles, Boats, Etc.:

Any Additional Comments:

After Recording Return To:

_____

_____

_____

_____

_____[Space Above This Line For Recording Data]_____

MORTGAGE

WORDS USED OFTEN IN THIS DOCUMENT

(A) **"Security Instrument."** This document, which is dated _____,
_____, together with all Riders to this document, will be called the "Security Instrument."
(B) **"Borrower."** _____,
whose address is _____
_____ sometimes will be called "Borrower" and sometimes simply "I" or "me."
(C) **"Lender."** _____
will be called "Lender." Lender is a corporation or association which exists under the laws of
_____. Lender's address is _____
_____.
(D) **"Note."** The note signed by Borrower and dated _____,
_____, will be called the "Note." The Note shows that I owe Lender _____
_____ Dollars (U.S. $_____)
plus interest and other amounts that may be payable. I have promised to pay this debt in Periodic
Payments and to pay the debt in full by _____, _____.
(E) **"Property."** The property that is described below in the section titled "Description of the
Property," will be called the "Property."
(F) **"Loan."** The "Loan" means the debt evidenced by the Note, plus interest, any
prepayment charges and late charges due under the Note, and all sums due under this Security
Instrument, plus interest.
(G) **"Sums Secured."** The amounts described below in the section titled "Borrower's
Transfer to Lender of Rights in the Property" sometimes will be called the "Sums Secured."

(H) "Riders." All Riders attached to this Security Instrument that are signed by Borrower will be called "Riders." The following Riders are to be signed by Borrower [check box as applicable]:

☐ Adjustable Rate Rider   ☐ Condominium Rider   ☐ Second Home Rider
☐ Balloon Rider   ☐ Planned Unit Development Rider   ☐ Other(s) [specify] _____
☐ 1-4 Family Rider   ☐ Biweekly Payment Rider

(I) "Applicable Law." All controlling applicable federal, state and local statutes, regulations, ordinances and administrative rules and orders (that have the effect of law) as well as all applicable final, non-appealable, judicial opinions will be called "Applicable Law."

(J) "Community Association Dues, Fees, and Assessments." All dues, fees, assessments, and other charges that are imposed on Borrower or the Property by a condominium association, homeowners association or similar organization will be called "Community Association Dues, Fees, and Assessments."

(K) "Electronic Funds Transfer." "Electronic Funds Transfer" means any transfer of money, other than by check, draft, or similar paper instrument, which is initiated through an electronic terminal, telephonic instrument, computer, or magnetic tape so as to order, instruct, or authorize a financial institution to debit or credit an account. Some common examples of an Electronic Funds Transfer are point-of-sale transfers (where a card such as an asset or debit card is used at a merchant), automated teller machine (or ATM) transactions, transfers initiated by telephone, wire transfers, and automated clearinghouse transfers.

(L) "Escrow Items." Those items that are described in Section 3 will be called "Escrow Items."

(M) "Miscellaneous Proceeds." "Miscellaneous Proceeds" means any compensation, settlement, award of damages, or proceeds paid by any third party (other than Insurance Proceeds, as defined in, and paid under the coverage described in, Section 5) for: (i) damage to, or destruction of, the Property; (ii) Condemnation or other taking of all or any part of the Property; (iii) conveyance in lieu of Condemnation or sale to avoid Condemnation; or (iv) misrepresentations of, or omissions as to, the value and/or condition of the Property. A taking of the Property by any governmental authority by eminent domain is known as "Condemnation."

(N) "Mortgage Insurance." "Mortgage Insurance" means insurance protecting Lender against the nonpayment of, or default on, the Loan.

(O) "Periodic Payment." The regularly scheduled amount due for (i) principal and interest under the Note, and (ii) any amounts under Section 3 will be called "Periodic Payment."

(P) "RESPA." "RESPA" means the Real Estate Settlement Procedures Act (12 U.S.C. §2601 et seq.) and its implementing regulation, Regulation X (24 C.F.R. Part 3500), as they might be amended from time to time, or any additional or successor legislation or regulation that governs the same subject matter. As used in this Security Instrument, "RESPA" refers to all requirements and restrictions that are imposed in regard to a "federally related mortgage loan" even if the Loan does not qualify as a "federally related mortgage loan" under RESPA.

BORROWER'S TRANSFER TO LENDER OF RIGHTS IN THE PROPERTY

I mortgage, grant and convey the Property to Lender subject to the terms of this Security Instrument. This means that, by signing this Security Instrument, I am giving Lender those rights that are stated in this Security Instrument and also those rights that Applicable Law gives to lenders who hold mortgages on real property. I am giving Lender these rights to protect Lender from possible losses that might result if I fail to:

(A)   Pay all the amounts that I owe Lender as stated in the Note including, but not limited to, all renewals, extensions and modifications of the Note;

(B)   Pay, with interest, any amounts that Lender spends under this Security Instrument to protect the value of the Property and Lender's rights in the Property; and

(C)   Keep all of my other promises and agreements under this Security Instrument and the Note.

DESCRIPTION OF THE PROPERTY

I give Lender rights in the Property described in (A) through (G) below:

(A)   The Property which is located at _____,
                                                          [Street]
_____, New York _____.
            [City, Town or Village]   [Zip Code]
This Property is in _____ County. It has the
following legal description:

(B)   All buildings and other improvements that are located on the Property described in subsection (A) of this section;

(C)   All rights in other property that I have as owner of the Property described in subsection (A) of this section. These rights are known as "easements and appurtenances attached to the Property;"

(D)   All rights that I have in the land which lies in the streets or roads in front of, or next to, the Property described in subsection (A) of this section;

(E)   All fixtures that are now or in the future will be on the Property described in subsections (A) and (B) of this section;

(F)   All of the rights and property described in subsections (B) through (E) of this section that I acquire in the future; and

(G)   All replacements of or additions to the Property described in subsections (B) through (F) of this section and all Insurance Proceeds for loss or damage to, and all Miscellaneous Proceeds of the Property described in subsections (A) through (F) of this section.

BORROWER'S RIGHT TO MORTGAGE THE PROPERTY AND BORROWER'S OBLIGATION TO DEFEND OWNERSHIP OF THE PROPERTY

I promise that: (A) I lawfully own the Property; (B) I have the right to mortgage, grant and convey the Property to Lender; and (C) there are no outstanding claims or charges against the Property, except for those which are of public record.

I give a general warranty of title to Lender. This means that I will be fully responsible for any losses which Lender suffers because someone other than myself has some of the rights in the Property which I promise that I have. I promise that I will defend my ownership of the Property against any claims of such rights.

PLAIN LANGUAGE SECURITY INSTRUMENT

This Security Instrument contains promises and agreements that are used in real property security instruments all over the country. It also contains other promises and agreements that vary in different parts of the country. My promises and agreements are stated in "plain language."

COVENANTS

I promise and I agree with Lender as follows:

1. **Borrower's Promise to Pay.** I will pay to Lender on time principal and interest due under the Note and any prepayment, late charges and other amounts due under the Note. I will also pay all amounts for Escrow Items under Section 3 of this Security Instrument.

Payments due under the Note and this Security Instrument shall be made in U.S. currency. If any of my payments by check or other payment instrument is returned to Lender unpaid, Lender may require my payment be made by: (a) cash; (b) money order; (c) certified check, bank check, treasurer's check or cashier's check, drawn upon an institution whose deposits are insured by a federal agency, instrumentality, or entity; or (d) Electronic Funds Transfer.

Payments are deemed received by Lender when received at the location required in the Note, or at another location designated by Lender under Section 15 of this Security Instrument. Lender may return or accept any payment or partial payment if it is for an amount that is less than the amount that is then due. If Lender accepts a lesser payment, Lender may refuse to accept a lesser payment that I may make in the future and does not waive any of its rights. Lender is not obligated to apply such lesser payments when it accepts such payments. If interest on principal accrues as if all Periodic Payments had been paid when due, then Lender need not pay interest on unapplied funds. Lender may hold such unapplied funds until I make payments to bring the Loan current. If I do not do so within a reasonable period of time, Lender will either apply such funds or return them to me. In the event of foreclosure, any unapplied funds will be applied to the outstanding principal balance immediately prior to foreclosure. No offset or claim which I might have now or in the future against Lender will relieve me from making payments due under the Note and this Security Instrument or keeping all of my other promises and agreements secured by this Security Instrument.

2. **Application of Borrower's Payments and Insurance Proceeds.** Unless Applicable Law or this Section 2 requires otherwise, Lender will apply each of my payments that Lender accepts in the following order:

First, to pay interest due under the Note;

Next, to pay principal due under the Note; and

Next, to pay the amounts due Lender under Section 3 of this Security Instrument.

Such payments will be applied to each Periodic Payment in the order in which it became due. Any remaining amounts will be applied as follows:

First, to pay any late charges;

Next, to pay any other amounts due under this Security Instrument; and

Next, to reduce the principal balance of the Note.

If Lender receives a payment from me for a late Periodic Payment which includes a sufficient amount to pay any late charge due, the payment may be applied to the late Periodic Payment and the late charge. If more than one Periodic Payment is due, Lender may apply any payment received from me: First, to the repayment of the Periodic Payments that are due if, and to the extent that, each payment can be paid in full; Next, to the extent that any excess exists after the payment is applied to the full payment of one or more Periodic Payments, such excess may be applied to any late charges due.

Voluntary prepayments will be applied as follows: First, to any prepayment charges; and Next, as described in the Note.

Any application of payments, Insurance Proceeds, or Miscellaneous Proceeds to principal due under the Note will not extend or postpone the due date of the Periodic Payments or change the amount of those payments.

3. **Monthly Payments For Taxes And Insurance.**

(a) **Borrower's Obligations.** I will pay to Lender all amounts necessary to pay for taxes, assessments, water charges, sewer rents and other similar charges, ground leasehold payments or rents (if any), hazard or property insurance covering the Property, flood insurance (if any), and any required Mortgage Insurance, or a Loss Reserve as described in Section 10 in the place of Mortgage Insurance. Each Periodic Payment will include an amount to be applied toward payment of the following items which are called "Escrow Items:"

(1) The taxes, assessments, water charges, sewer rents and other similar charges, on the Property which under Applicable Law may be superior to this Security Instrument as a Lien on the Property. Any claim, demand or charge that is made against property because an obligation has not been fulfilled is known as a "Lien;"

(2) The leasehold payments or ground rents on the Property (if any);

(3) The premium for any and all insurance required by Lender under Section 5 of this Security Instrument;

(4) The premium for Mortgage Insurance (if any);

(5) The amount I may be required to pay Lender under Section 10 of this Security Instrument instead of the payment of the premium for Mortgage Insurance (if any); and

(6) If required by Lender, the amount for any Community Association Dues, Fees, and Assessments.

After signing the Note, or at any time during its term, Lender may include these amounts as Escrow Items. The monthly payment I will make for Escrow Items will be based on Lender's estimate of the annual amount required.

I will pay all of these amounts to Lender unless Lender tells me, in writing, that I do not have to do so, or unless Applicable Law requires otherwise. I will make these payments on the same day that my Periodic Payments of principal and interest are due under the Note.

The amounts that I pay to Lender for Escrow Items under this Section 3 will be called "Escrow Funds." I will pay Lender the Escrow Funds for Escrow Items unless Lender waives my obligation to pay the Escrow Funds for any or all Escrow Items. Lender may waive my obligation to pay to Lender Escrow Funds for any or all Escrow Items at any time. Any such waiver must be in writing. In the event of such waiver, I will pay directly, when and where payable, the amounts due for any Escrow Items for which payment of Escrow Funds has been waived by Lender and, if Lender requires, will promptly send to Lender receipts showing such payment within such time period as Lender may require. My obligation to make such payments and to provide receipts will be considered to be a promise and agreement contained in this Security Instrument, as the phrase "promises and agreements" is used in Section 9 of this Security Instrument. If I am obligated to pay Escrow Items directly, pursuant to a waiver, and I fail to pay the amount due for an Escrow Item, Lender may pay that amount and I will then be obligated under Section 9 of this Security Instrument to repay to Lender. Lender may revoke the waiver as to any or all Escrow Items at any time by a notice given in accordance with Section 15 of this Security Instrument and, upon the revocation, I will pay to Lender all Escrow Funds, and in amounts, that are then required under this Section 3.

I promise to promptly send to Lender any notices that I receive of Escrow Item amounts to be paid. Lender will estimate from time to time the amount of Escrow Funds I will have to pay by using existing assessments and bills and reasonable estimates of the amount I will have to pay for Escrow Items in the future, unless Applicable Law requires Lender to use another method for determining the amount I am to pay.

Lender may, at any time, collect and hold Escrow Funds in an amount sufficient to permit Lender to apply the Escrow Funds at the time specified under RESPA. Applicable Law puts limits on the total amount of Escrow Funds Lender can at any time collect and hold. This total amount cannot be more than the maximum amount a lender could require under RESPA. If there is another Applicable Law that imposes a lower limit on the total amount of Escrow Funds Lender can collect and hold, Lender will be limited to the lower amount.

(b) **Lender's Obligations.** Lender will keep the Escrow Funds in a savings or banking institution which has its deposits insured by a federal agency, instrumentality, or entity, or in any Federal Home Loan Bank. If Lender is such a savings or banking institution, Lender may hold the Escrow Funds. Lender will use the Escrow Funds to pay the Escrow Items no later than the time allowed under RESPA or other Applicable Law. Lender will give to me, without charge, an annual accounting of the Escrow Funds. That accounting will show all additions to and deductions from the Escrow Funds and the reason for each deduction.

Lender may not charge me for holding or keeping the Escrow Funds, for using the Escrow Funds to pay Escrow Items, for making a yearly analysis of my payment of Escrow Funds or for receiving, or for verifying and totaling assessments and bills. However, Lender may charge me for these services if Lender pays me interest on the Escrow Funds and if Applicable Law permits Lender to make such a charge. Lender will not be required to pay me any interest or earnings on the Escrow Funds unless either (1) Lender and I agree in writing that Lender will pay interest on the Escrow Funds, or (2) Applicable Law requires Lender to pay interest on the Escrow Funds.

(c)   **Adjustments to the Escrow Funds**. Under Applicable Law, there is a limit on the amount of Escrow Funds Lender may hold. If the amount of Escrow Funds held by Lender exceeds this limit, then there will be an excess amount and RESPA requires Lender to account to me in a special manner for the excess amount of Escrow Funds.

If, at any time, Lender has not received enough Escrow Funds to make the payments of Escrow Items when the payments are due, Lender may tell me in writing that an additional amount is necessary. I will pay to Lender whatever additional amount is necessary to pay the Escrow Items when the payments are due, but the number of payments will not be more than 12.

When I have paid all of the Sums Secured, Lender will promptly refund to me any Escrow Funds that are then being held by Lender.

4.   **Borrower's Obligation to Pay Charges, Assessments And Claims.** I will pay all taxes, assessments, water charges, sewer rents and other similar charges, and any other charges and fines that may be imposed on the Property and that may be superior to this Security Instrument. I will also make ground rents or payments due under my lease if I am a tenant on the Property and Community Association Dues, Fees, and Assessments (if any) due on the Property. If these items are Escrow Items, I will do this by making the payments as described in Section 3 of this Security Instrument. In this Security Instrument, the word "Person" means any individual, organization, governmental authority or other party.

I will promptly pay or satisfy all Liens against the Property that may be superior to this Security Instrument. However, this Security Instrument does not require me to satisfy a superior Lien if: (a) I agree, in writing, to pay the obligation which gave rise to the superior Lien and Lender approves the way in which I agree to pay that obligation, but only so long as I am performing such agreement; (b) in good faith, I argue or defend against the superior Lien in a lawsuit so that in Lender's opinion, during the lawsuit, the superior Lien may not be enforced, but only until the lawsuit ends; or (c) I secure from the holder of that other Lien an agreement, approved in writing by Lender, that the Lien of this Security Instrument is superior to the Lien held by that Person. If Lender determines that any part of the Property is subject to a superior Lien, Lender may give Borrower a notice identifying the superior Lien. Within 10 days of the date on which the notice is given, Borrower shall pay or satisfy the superior Lien or take one or more of the actions mentioned in this Section 4.

Lender also may require me to pay a one-time charge for an independent real estate tax reporting service used by Lender in connection with the Loan, unless Applicable Law does not permit Lender to make such a charge.

5.   **Borrower's Obligation to Maintain Hazard Insurance or Property Insurance.** I will obtain hazard or property insurance to cover all buildings and other improvements that now are, or in the future will be, located on the Property. The insurance will cover loss or damage caused by fire, hazards normally covered by "Extended Coverage" hazard insurance policies, and any other hazards for which Lender requires coverage, including, but not limited to earthquakes and floods. The insurance will be in the amounts (including, but not limited to, deductible levels) and for the periods of time required by Lender. What Lender requires under the last sentence can change during the term of the Loan. I may choose the insurance company, but my choice is subject to Lender's right to disapprove. Lender may not disapprove my choice unless the disapproval is reasonable. Lender may require me to pay either (a) a one-time charge for flood zone determination, certification and tracking services, or (b) a one-time charge for flood zone determination and certification services and subsequent charges

each time remappings or similar changes occur which reasonably might affect the flood zone determination or certification. If I disagree with the flood zone determination, I may request the Federal Emergency Management Agency to review the flood zone determination and I promise to pay any fees charged by the Federal Emergency Management Agency for its review.

If I fail to maintain any of the insurance coverages described above, Lender may obtain insurance coverage, at Lender's option and my expense. Lender is under no obligation to purchase any particular type or amount of coverage. Therefore, such coverage will cover Lender, but might or might not protect me, my equity in the Property, or the contents of the Property, against any risk, hazard or liability and might provide greater or lesser coverage than was previously in effect. I acknowledge that the cost of the insurance coverage so obtained might significantly exceed the cost of insurance that I could have obtained. Any amounts disbursed by Lender under this Section 5 will become my additional debt secured by this Security Instrument. These amounts will bear interest at the interest rate set forth in the Note from the date of disbursement and will be payable with such interest, upon notice from Lender to me requesting payment.

All of the insurance policies and renewals of those policies will include what is known as a "Standard Mortgage Clause" to protect Lender and will name Lender as mortgagee and/or as an additional loss payee. The form of all policies and renewals will be acceptable to Lender. Lender will have the right to hold the policies and renewal certificates. If Lender requires, I will promptly give Lender all receipts of paid premiums and renewal notices that I receive.

If I obtain any form of insurance coverage, not otherwise required by Lender, for damage to, or destruction of, the Property, such policy will include a Standard Mortgage Clause and will name Lender as mortgagee and/or as an additional loss payee.

If there is a loss or damage to the Property, I will promptly notify the insurance company and Lender. If I do not promptly prove to the insurance company that the loss or damage occurred, then Lender may do so.

The amount paid by the insurance company for loss or damage to the Property is called "Insurance Proceeds." Unless Lender and I otherwise agree in writing, any Insurance Proceeds, whether or not the underlying insurance was required by Lender, will be used to repair or to restore the damaged Property unless: (a) it is not economically feasible to make the repairs or restoration; (b) the use of the Insurance Proceeds for that purpose would lessen the protection given to Lender by this Security Instrument; or (c) Lender and I have agreed in writing not to use the Insurance Proceeds for that purpose. During the period that any repairs or restorations are being made, Lender may hold any Insurance Proceeds until it has had an opportunity to inspect the Property to verify that the repair work has been completed to Lender's satisfaction. However, this inspection will be done promptly. Lender may make payments for the repairs and restorations in a single payment or in a series of progress payments as the work is completed. Unless Lender and I agree otherwise in writing or unless Applicable Law requires otherwise, Lender is not required to pay me any interest or earnings on the Insurance Proceeds. I will pay for any public adjusters or other third parties that I hire, and their fees will not be paid out of the Insurance Proceeds. If the repair or restoration is not economically feasible or if it would lessen Lender's protection under this Security Instrument, then the Insurance Proceeds will be used to reduce the amount that I owe to Lender under this Security Instrument. Such Insurance Proceeds will be applied in the order provided for in Section 2. If any of the Insurance Proceeds remain after the amount that I owe to Lender has been paid in full, the remaining Insurance Proceeds will be paid to me.

If I abandon the Property, Lender may file, negotiate and settle any available insurance claim and related matters. If I do not answer, within 30 days, a notice from Lender stating that the insurance company has offered to settle a claim, Lender may negotiate and settle the claim. The 30-day period will begin when the notice is given. In either event, or if Lender acquires the Property under Section 22 of this Security Instrument or otherwise, I give Lender my rights to any Insurance Proceeds in an amount not greater than the amounts unpaid under the Note and this Security Instrument. I also give Lender any other of my rights (other than the right to any refund of unearned premiums that I paid) under all insurance policies covering the Property, if the rights are applicable to the coverage of the Property. Lender may use the Insurance Proceeds either to repair or restore the Property or to pay amounts unpaid under the Note or this Security Instrument, whether or not then due.

6. **Borrower's Obligations to Occupy The Property.** I will occupy the Property and use the Property as my principal residence within 60 days after I sign this Security Instrument. I will continue to occupy the Property and to use the Property as my principal residence for at least one year. The one-year period will begin when I first occupy the Property. However, I will not have to occupy the Property and use the Property as my principal residence within the time frames set forth above if Lender agrees in writing that I do not have to do so. Lender may not refuse to agree unless the refusal is reasonable. I also will not have to occupy the Property and use the Property as my principal residence within the time frames set forth above if extenuating circumstances exist which are beyond my control.

7. **Borrower's Obligations to Maintain And Protect The Property And to Fulfill Any Lease Obligations.**

(a) **Maintenance and Protection of the Property.** I will not destroy, damage or harm the Property, and I will not allow the Property to deteriorate. Whether or not I am residing in the Property, I will keep the Property in good repair so that it will not deteriorate or decrease in value due to its condition. Unless it is determined under Section 5 of this Security Instrument that repair is not economically feasible, I will promptly repair the Property if damaged to avoid further deterioration or damage. If insurance or Condemnation (as defined in the definition of Miscellaneous Proceeds) proceeds are paid because of loss or damage to, or Condemnation of, the Property, I will repair or restore the Property only if Lender has released those proceeds for such purposes. Lender may pay for the repairs and restoration out of proceeds in a single payment or in a series of progress payments as the work is completed. If the insurance or Condemnation proceeds are not sufficient to repair or restore the Property, I promise to pay for the completion of such repair or restoration.

(b) **Lender's Inspection of Property.** Lender, and others authorized by Lender, may enter on and inspect the Property. They will do so in a reasonable manner and at reasonable times. If it has a reasonable purpose, Lender may inspect the inside of the home or other improvements on the Property. Before or at the time an inspection is made, Lender will give me notice stating a reasonable purpose for such interior inspection.

8. **Borrower's Loan Application.** If, during the application process for the Loan, I, or any Person or entity acting at my direction or with my knowledge or consent, made false, misleading, or inaccurate statements to Lender about information important to Lender in determining my eligibility for the Loan (or did not provide Lender with such information),

Lender will treat my actions as a default under this Security Instrument. False, misleading, or inaccurate statements about information important to Lender would include a misrepresentation of my intention to occupy the Property as a principal residence. This is just one example of a false, misleading, or inaccurate statement of important information.

9.   Lender's Right to Protect Its Rights in The Property. If: (a) I do not keep my promises and agreements made in this Security Instrument; (b) someone, including me, begins a legal proceeding that may significantly affect Lender's interest in the Property or rights under this Security Instrument (such as a legal proceeding in bankruptcy, in probate, for Condemnation or Forfeiture (as defined in Section 11), proceedings which could give a Person rights which could equal or exceed Lender's interest in the Property or under this Security Instrument, proceedings for enforcement of a Lien which may become superior to this Security Instrument, or to enforce laws or regulations); or (c) I have abandoned the Property, then Lender may do and pay for whatever is reasonable or appropriate to protect Lender's interest in the Property and Lender's rights under this Security Instrument.

Lender's actions may include, but are not limited to: (a) protecting and/or assessing the value of the Property; (b) securing and/or repairing the Property; (c) paying sums to eliminate any Lien against the Property that may be equal or superior to this Security Instrument; (d) appearing in court; and (e) paying reasonable attorneys' fees to protect its interest in the Property and/or rights under this Security Instrument, including its secured position in a bankruptcy proceeding. Lender can also enter the Property to make repairs, change locks, replace or board up doors and windows, drain water from pipes, eliminate building or other code violations or dangerous conditions, have utilities turned on or off, and take any other action to secure the Property. Although Lender may take action under this Section 9, Lender does not have to do so and is under no duty to do so. I agree that Lender will not be liable for not taking any or all actions under this Section 9.

I will pay to Lender any amounts, with interest, which Lender spends under this Section 9. I will pay those amounts to Lender when Lender sends me a notice requesting that I do so. I will pay interest on those amounts at the interest rate set forth in the Note. Interest on each amount will begin on the date that the amount is spent by Lender. This Security Instrument will protect Lender in case I do not keep this promise to pay those amounts with interest.

If I do not own, but am a tenant on the Property, I will fulfill all my obligations under my lease. I also agree that, if I acquire the full title (sometimes called "Fee Title") to the Property, my lease interest and the Fee Title will not merge unless Lender agrees to the merger in writing.

10.   Mortgage Insurance. If Lender required Mortgage Insurance as a condition of making the Loan, I will pay the premiums for the Mortgage Insurance. If, for any reason, the Mortgage Insurance coverage ceases to be available from the mortgage insurer that previously provided such insurance and Lender required me to make separate payments toward the premiums for Mortgage Insurance, I will pay the premiums for substantially equivalent Mortgage Insurance coverage from an alternate mortgage insurer. However, the cost of this Mortgage Insurance coverage will be substantially equivalent to the cost to me of the previous Mortgage Insurance coverage, and the alternate mortgage insurer will be selected by Lender.

If substantially equivalent Mortgage Insurance coverage is not available, Lender will establish a non-refundable "Loss Reserve" as a substitute for the Mortgage Insurance coverage. I will continue to pay to Lender each month an amount equal to one-twelfth of the yearly Mortgage Insurance premium (as of the time the coverage lapsed or ceased to be in effect). Lender will retain these payments, and will use these payments to pay for losses that the Mortgage Insurance would have covered. The Loss Reserve is non-refundable even if the Loan is ultimately paid in full and Lender is not required to pay me any interest on the Loss Reserve. Lender can no longer require Loss Reserve payments if: (a) Mortgage Insurance coverage again becomes available through an insurer selected by Lender; (b) such Mortgage Insurance is obtained; (c) Lender requires separately designated payments toward the premiums for Mortgage Insurance; and (d) the Mortgage Insurance coverage is in the amount and for the period of time required by Lender.

If Lender required Mortgage Insurance as a condition of making the Loan and Borrower was required to make separate payments toward the premiums for Mortgage Insurance, I will pay the Mortgage Insurance premiums, or the Loss Reserve payments, until the requirement for Mortgage Insurance ends according to any written agreement between Lender and me providing for such termination or until termination of Mortgage Insurance is required by Applicable Law. Lender may require me to pay the premiums, or the Loss Reserve payments, in the manner described in Section 3 of this Security Instrument. Nothing in this Section 10 will affect my obligation to pay interest at the rate provided in the Note.

A Mortgage Insurance policy pays Lender (or any entity that purchases the Note) for certain losses it may incur if Borrower does not repay the Loan as agreed. Borrower is not a party to the Mortgage Insurance policy.

Mortgage insurers assess their total risk on all Mortgage Insurance from time to time. Mortgage insurers may enter into agreements with other parties to share or change their risk, or to reduce losses. These agreements are based on terms and conditions that are satisfactory to the mortgage insurer and the other party (or parties) to these agreements. These agreements may require the mortgage insurer to make payments using any source of funds that the mortgage insurer may have available (which may include Mortgage Insurance premiums).

As a result of these agreements, Lender, any owner of the Note, another insurer, any reinsurer, or any other entity, may receive (directly or indirectly) amounts that come from a portion of Borrower's payments for Mortgage Insurance, in exchange for sharing or changing the mortgage insurer's risk, or reducing losses. If these agreements provide that an affiliate of Lender takes a share of the insurer's risk in exchange for a share of the premiums paid to the insurer, the arrangement is often termed "captive reinsurance."

It also should be understood that: (a) any of these agreements will not affect the amounts that Borrower has agreed to pay for Mortgage Insurance, or any other terms of the Loan. These agreements will not increase the amount Borrower will owe for Mortgage Insurance, and they will not entitle Borrower to any refund; and (b) any of these agreements will not affect the rights Borrower has – if any – regarding the Mortgage Insurance under the Homeowners Protection Act of 1998 or any other law. These rights may include the right (a) to receive certain disclosures, (b) to request and obtain cancellation of the Mortgage Insurance, (c) to have the Mortgage Insurance terminated automatically, and/or (d) to receive a refund of any Mortgage Insurance premiums that were not earned at the time of such cancellation or termination.

   11.   Agreements About Miscellaneous Proceeds; Forfeiture. All Miscellaneous Proceeds are assigned to and will be paid to Lender.

If the Property is damaged, such Miscellaneous Proceeds will be applied to restoration or repair of the Property, if (a) the restoration or repair is economically feasible, and (b) Lender's security given in this Security Instrument is not lessened. During such repair and restoration period, Lender will have the right to hold such Miscellaneous Proceeds until Lender has had an opportunity to inspect the Property to verify that the work has been completed to Lender's satisfaction. However, the inspection will be undertaken promptly. Lender may pay for the repairs and restoration in a single disbursement or in a series of progress payments as the work is completed. Unless Lender and I agree otherwise in writing or unless Applicable Law requires interest to be paid on such Miscellaneous Proceeds, Lender will not be required to pay Borrower any interest or earnings on the Miscellaneous Proceeds. If the restoration or repair is not economically feasible or Lender's security given in this Security Instrument would be lessened, the Miscellaneous Proceeds will be applied to the Sums Secured, whether or not then due. The excess, if any, will be paid to me. Such Miscellaneous Proceeds will be applied in the order provided for in Section 2.

In the event of a total taking, destruction, or loss in value of the Property, the Miscellaneous Proceeds will be applied to the Sums Secured, whether or not then due. The excess, if any, will be paid to me.

In the event of a partial taking, destruction, or loss in value of the Property in which the fair market value of the Property immediately before the partial taking, destruction, or loss in value is equal to or greater than the amount of the Sums Secured immediately before the partial taking, destruction, or loss in value, the Sums Secured will be reduced by the amount of the Miscellaneous Proceeds multiplied by the following fraction: (a) the total amount of the Sums Secured immediately before the partial taking, destruction, or loss in value divided by (b) the fair market value of the Property immediately before the partial taking, destruction, or loss in value. Any balance shall be paid to me.

In the event of a partial taking, destruction, or loss in value of the Property in which the fair market value of the Property immediately before the partial taking, destruction, or loss in value is less than the amount of the Sums Secured immediately before the partial taking, destruction, or loss in value, the Miscellaneous Proceeds will be applied to the Sums Secured whether or not the sums are then due.

If I abandon the Property, or if, after Lender sends me notice that the Opposing Party (as defined in the next sentence) offered to make an award to settle a claim for damages, I fail to respond to Lender within 30 days after the date Lender gives notice, Lender is authorized to collect and apply the Miscellaneous Proceeds either to restoration or repair of the Property or to the Sums Secured, whether or not then due. "Opposing Party" means the third party that owes me Miscellaneous Proceeds or the party against whom I have a right of action in regard to Miscellaneous Proceeds.

I will be in default under this Security Instrument if any civil or criminal action or proceeding that Lender determines could result in a court ruling (a) that would require Forfeiture of the Property, or (b) that could damage Lender's interest in the Property or rights under this Security Instrument. "Forfeiture" is a court action to require the Property, or any part of the Property, to be given up. I may correct the default by obtaining a court ruling that dismisses the court action, if Lender determines that this court ruling prevents Forfeiture of the Property and also prevents any damage to Lender's interest in the Property or rights under this Security Instrument. If I correct the default, I will have the right to have enforcement of this Security Instrument discontinued, as provided in Section 19 of this Security Instrument, even if Lender has required Immediate Payment in Full (as defined in Section 22). The proceeds of any award or claim for damages that are attributable to the damage or reduction of Lender's interest in the Property are assigned, and will be paid, to Lender.

All Miscellaneous Proceeds that are not applied to restoration or repair of the Property will be applied in the order provided for in Section 2.

12.   Continuation of Borrower's Obligations And of Lender's Rights.

(a)   Borrower's Obligations. Lender may allow me, or a Person who takes over my rights and obligations, to delay or to change the amount of the Periodic Payments. Even if Lender does this, however, I will still be fully obligated under the Note and under this Security Instrument unless Lender agrees to release me, in writing, from my obligations.

Lender may allow those delays or changes for me or a Person who takes over my rights and obligations, even if Lender is requested not to do so. Even if Lender is requested to do so, Lender will not be required to (1) bring a lawsuit against me or such a Person for not fulfilling obligations under the Note or under this Security Instrument, or (2) refuse to extend time for payment or otherwise modify amortization of the Sums Secured.

(b)   Lender's Rights. Even if Lender does not exercise or enforce any right of Lender under this Security Instrument or under Applicable Law, Lender will still have all of those rights and may exercise and enforce them in the future. Even if: (1) Lender obtains insurance, pays taxes, or pays other claims, charges or Liens against the Property; (2) Lender accepts payments from third Persons; or (3) Lender accepts payments in amounts less than the amount then due, Lender will have the right under Section 22 below to demand that I make Immediate Payment in Full of any amounts remaining due and payable to Lender under the Note and under this Security Instrument.

13.   Obligations of Borrower And of Persons Taking Over Borrower's Rights or Obligations. If more than one Person signs this Security Instrument as Borrower, each of us is fully obligated to keep all of Borrower's promises and obligations contained in this Security Instrument. Lender may enforce Lender's rights under this Security Instrument against each of us individually or against all of us together. This means that any one of us may be required to pay all of the Sums Secured. However, if one of us does not sign the Note: (a) that Person is signing this Security Instrument only to give that Person's rights in the Property to Lender under the terms of this Security Instrument; (b) that Person is not personally obligated to pay the Sums Secured; and (c) that Person agrees that Lender may agree with the other Borrowers to delay enforcing any of Lender's rights, to modify, or make any accommodations with regard to the terms of this Security Instrument or the Note without that Person's consent.

Subject to the provisions of Section 18 of this Security Instrument, any Person who takes over my rights or obligations under this Security Instrument in writing, and is approved by Lender in writing, will have all of my rights and will be obligated to keep all of my promises and agreements made in this Security Instrument. Borrower will not be released from Borrower's obligations and liabilities under this Security Instrument unless Lender agrees to such release in writing. Any Person who takes over Lender's rights or obligations under this Security Instrument will have all of Lender's rights and will be obligated to keep all of Lender's promises and agreements made in this Security Instrument except as provided under Section 20.

14.   Loan Charges. Lender may charge me fees for services performed in connection with my default, for the purpose of protecting Lender's interest in the Property and rights under this Security Instrument, including, but not limited to, attorneys' fees, property inspection and valuation fees. With regard to other fees, the fact that this Security Instrument does not expressly indicate that Lender may charge a certain fee does not mean that Lender cannot charge that fee. Lender may not charge fees that are prohibited by this Security Instrument or by Applicable Law.

If the Loan is subject to Applicable Law which sets maximum loan charges, and that Applicable Law is finally interpreted so that the interest or other loan charges collected or to be collected in connection with the Loan exceed permitted limits: (a) any such loan charge will be reduced by the amount necessary to reduce the charge to the permitted limit; and (b) any sums already collected from me which exceeded permitted limits will be refunded to me. Lender may choose to make this refund by reducing the principal owed under the Note or by making a direct payment to Borrower. If a refund reduces principal, the reduction will be treated as a partial prepayment without any prepayment charge (even if a prepayment charge is provided for under the Note). If I accept such a refund that is paid directly to me, I will waive any right to bring a lawsuit against Lender because of the overcharge.

   15.   Notices Required under this Security Instrument. All notices given by me or Lender in connection with this Security Instrument will be in writing. Any notice to me in connection with this Security Instrument is considered given to me when mailed by first class mail or when actually delivered to my notice address if sent by other means. Notice to any one Borrower will be notice to all Borrowers unless Applicable Law expressly requires otherwise. The notice address is the address of the Property unless I give notice to Lender of a different address. I will promptly notify Lender of my change of address. If Lender specifies a procedure for reporting my change of address, then I will only report a change of address through that specified procedure. There may be only one designated notice address under this Security Instrument at any one time. Any notice to Lender will be given by delivering it or by mailing it by first class mail to Lender's address stated on the first page of this Security Instrument unless Lender has given me notice of another address. Any notice in connection with this Security Instrument is given to Lender when it is actually received by Lender. If any notice required by this Security Instrument is also required under Applicable Law, the Applicable Law requirement will satisfy the corresponding requirement under this Security Instrument.

   16.   Law That Governs this Security Instrument; Word Usage. This Security Instrument is governed by federal law and the law of New York State. All rights and obligations contained in this Security Instrument are subject to any requirements and limitations of Applicable Law. Applicable Law might allow the parties to agree by contract or it might be silent, but such silence does not mean that Lender and I cannot agree by contract. If any term of this Security Instrument or of the Note conflicts with Applicable Law, the conflict will not affect other provisions of this Security Instrument or the Note which can operate, or be given effect, without the conflicting provision. This means that the Security Instrument or the Note will remain as if the conflicting provision did not exist.

   As used in this Security Instrument: (a) words of the masculine gender mean and include corresponding words of the feminine and neuter genders; (b) words in the singular mean and include the plural, and words in the plural mean and include the singular; and (c) the word "may" gives sole discretion without any obligation to take any action.

   17.   Borrower's Copy. I will be given one copy of the Note and of this Security Instrument.

   18.   Agreements about Lender's Rights If the Property Is Sold or Transferred. Lender may require Immediate Payment in Full of all Sums Secured by this Security Instrument if all or any part of the Property, or if any right in the Property, is sold or transferred without Lender's prior written permission. If Borrower is not a natural Person and a beneficial interest in Borrower is sold or transferred without Lender's prior written permission, Lender also may require Immediate Payment in Full. However, this option shall not be exercised by Lender if such exercise is prohibited by Applicable Law.

If Lender requires Immediate Payment in Full under this Section 18, Lender will give me a notice which states this requirement. The notice will give me at least 30 days to make the required payment. The 30-day period will begin on the date the notice is given to me in the manner required by Section 15 of this Security Instrument. If I do not make the required payment during that period, Lender may act to enforce its rights under this Security Instrument without giving me any further notice or demand for payment.

19. Borrower's Right to Have Lender's Enforcement of this Security Instrument Discontinued. Even if Lender has required Immediate Payment in Full, I may have the right to have enforcement of this Security Instrument stopped. I will have this right at any time before the earliest of: (a) five days before sale of the Property under any power of sale granted by this Security Instrument; (b) another period as Applicable Law might specify for the termination of my right to have enforcement of the Loan stopped; or (c) a judgment has been entered enforcing this Security Instrument. In order to have this right, I will meet the following conditions:

(a)   I pay to Lender the full amount that then would be due under this Security Instrument and the Note as if Immediate Payment in Full had never been required;

(b)   I correct my failure to keep any of my other promises or agreements made in this Security Instrument;

(c)   I pay all of Lender's reasonable expenses in enforcing this Security Instrument including, for example, reasonable attorneys' fees, property inspection and valuation fees, and other fees incurred for the purpose of protecting Lender's interest in the Property and rights under this Security Instrument; and

(d)   I do whatever Lender reasonably requires to assure that Lender's interest in the Property and rights under this Security Instrument and my obligations under the Note and under this Security Instrument continue unchanged.

Lender may require that I pay the sums and expenses mentioned in (a) through (d) in one or more of the following forms, as selected by Lender: (a) cash; (b) money order; (c) certified check, bank check, treasurer's check or cashier's check drawn upon an institution whose deposits are insured by a federal agency, instrumentality or entity; or (d) Electronic Funds Transfer.

If I fulfill all of the conditions in this Section 19, then this Security Instrument will remain in full effect as if Immediate Payment in Full had never been required. However, I will not have the right to have Lender's enforcement of this Security Instrument discontinued if Lender has required Immediate Payment in Full under Section 18 of this Security Instrument.

20. Note Holder's Right to Sell the Note or an Interest in the Note; Borrower's Right to Notice of Change of Loan Servicer; Lender's and Borrower's Right to Notice of Grievance. The Note, or an interest in the Note, together with this Security Instrument, may be sold one or more times. I might not receive any prior notice of these sales.

The entity that collects the Periodic Payments and performs other mortgage loan servicing obligations under the Note, this Security Instrument, and Applicable Law is called the "Loan Servicer." There may be a change of the Loan Servicer as a result of the sale of the Note. There also may be one or more changes of the Loan Servicer unrelated to a sale of the Note. Applicable Law requires that I be given written notice of any change of the Loan Servicer. The notice will state the name and address of the new Loan Servicer, and also tell me the address to which I should make my payments. The notice also will contain any other information required by RESPA or Applicable Law. If the Note is sold and thereafter the Loan is serviced by a Loan Servicer other than the purchaser of the Note, the mortgage loan servicing obligations to me will remain with the Loan Servicer or be transferred to a successor Loan Servicer and are not assumed by the Note purchaser unless otherwise provided by the Note purchaser.

Neither I nor Lender may commence, join or be joined to any court action (as either an individual party or the member of a class) that arises from the other party's actions pursuant to this Security Instrument or that alleges that the other has not fulfilled any of its obligations under this Security Instrument, unless the other is notified (in the manner required under Section 15 of this Security Instrument) of the unfulfilled obligation and given a reasonable time period to take corrective action. If Applicable Law provides a time period which will elapse before certain action can be taken, that time period will be deemed to be reasonable for purposes of this paragraph. The notice of acceleration and opportunity to cure given to me under Section 22 and the notice of the demand for payment in full given to me under Section 22 will be deemed to satisfy the notice and opportunity to take corrective action provisions of this Section 20. All rights under this paragraph are subject to Applicable Law.

21.   Continuation of Borrower's Obligations to Maintain and Protect the Property. The federal laws and the laws of New York State that relate to health, safety or environmental protection are called "Environmental Law." Environmental Law classifies certain substances as toxic or hazardous. There are other substances that are considered hazardous for purposes of this Section 21. These substances are gasoline, kerosene, other flammable or toxic petroleum products, toxic pesticides and herbicides, volatile solvents, materials containing asbestos or formaldehyde, and radioactive materials. The substances defined as toxic or hazardous by Environmental Law and the substances considered hazardous for purposes of this Section 21 are called "Hazardous Substances." "Environmental Cleanup" includes any response action, remedial action, or removal action, as defined in Environmental Law. An "Environmental Condition" means a condition that can cause, contribute to, or otherwise trigger an Environmental Cleanup.

I will not do anything affecting the Property that violates Environmental Law, and I will not allow anyone else to do so. I will not cause or permit Hazardous Substances to be present on the Property. I will not use or store Hazardous Substances on the Property. I also will not dispose of Hazardous Substances on the Property, or release any Hazardous Substance on the Property, and I will not allow anyone else to do so. I also will not do, nor allow anyone else to do, anything affecting the Property that: (a) is in violation of any Environmental Law; (b) creates an Environmental Condition; or (c) which, due to the presence, use, or release of a Hazardous Substance, creates a condition that adversely affects the value of the Property. The promises in this paragraph do not apply to the presence, use, or storage on the Property of small quantities of Hazardous Substances that are generally recognized as appropriate for normal residential use and maintenance of the Property (including, but not limited to, Hazardous Substances in consumer products). I may use or store these small quantities on the Property. In addition, unless Environmental Law requires removal or other action, the buildings, the improvements and the fixtures on the Property are permitted to contain asbestos and asbestos-containing materials if the asbestos and asbestos-containing materials are undisturbed and "non-friable" (that is, not easily crumbled by hand pressure).

I will promptly give Lender written notice of: (a) any investigation, claim, demand, lawsuit or other action by any governmental or regulatory agency or private party involving the

Property and any Hazardous Substance or Environmental Law of which I have actual knowledge; (b) any Environmental Condition, including but not limited to, any spilling, leaking, discharge, release or threat of release of any Hazardous Substance; and (c) any condition caused by the presence, use or release of a Hazardous Substance which adversely affects the value of the Property. If I learn, or any governmental or regulatory authority, or any private party, notifies me that any removal or other remediation of any Hazardous Substance affecting the Property is necessary, I will promptly take all necessary remedial actions in accordance with Environmental Law.

Nothing in this Security Instrument creates an obligation on Lender for an Environmental Cleanup.

NON-UNIFORM COVENANTS

I also promise and agree with Lender as follows:

22. **Lender's Rights If Borrower Fails to Keep Promises and Agreements. Except as provided in Section 18 of this Security Instrument, if all of the conditions stated in subsections (a), (b) and (c) of this Section 22 are met, Lender may require that I pay immediately the entire amount then remaining unpaid under the Note and under this Security Instrument. Lender may do this without making any further demand for payment. This requirement is called "Immediate Payment in Full."**

If Lender requires Immediate Payment in Full, Lender may bring a lawsuit to take away all of my remaining rights in the Property and have the Property sold. At this sale Lender or another Person may acquire the Property. This is known as "Foreclosure and Sale." In any lawsuit for Foreclosure and Sale, Lender will have the right to collect all costs and disbursements and additional allowances allowed by Applicable Law and will have the right to add all reasonable attorneys' fees to the amount I owe Lender, which fees shall become part of the Sums Secured.

Lender may require Immediate Payment in Full under this Section 22 only if all of the following conditions are met:

(a) **I fail to keep any promise or agreement made in this Security Instrument or the Note, including, but not limited to, the promises to pay the Sums Secured when due, or if another default occurs under this Security Instrument;**

(b) **Lender sends to me, in the manner described in Section 15 of this Security Instrument, a notice that states:**

(1) **The promise or agreement that I failed to keep or the default that has occurred;**

(2) **The action that I must take to correct that default;**

(3) **A date by which I must correct the default. That date will be at least 30 days from the date on which the notice is given;**

(4) **That if I do not correct the default by the date stated in the notice, Lender may require Immediate Payment in Full, and Lender or another Person may acquire the Property by means of Foreclosure and Sale;**

(5) **That if I meet the conditions stated in Section 19 of this Security Instrument, I will have the right to have Lender's enforcement of this Security Instrument stopped and to have the Note and this Security**

Instrument remain fully effective as if Immediate Payment in Full had never been required; and

(6) That I have the right in any lawsuit for Foreclosure and Sale to argue that I did keep my promises and agreements under the Note and under this Security Instrument, and to present any other defenses that I may have; and

(c) I do not correct the default stated in the notice from Lender by the date stated in that notice.

23. Lender's Obligation to Discharge this Security Instrument. When Lender has been paid all amounts due under the Note and under this Security Instrument, Lender will discharge this Security Instrument by delivering a certificate stating that this Security Instrument has been satisfied. I will pay all costs of recording the discharge in the proper official records. I agree to pay a fee for the discharge of this Security Instrument, if Lender so requires. Lender may require that I pay such a fee, but only if the fee is paid to a third party for services rendered and the charging of the fee is permitted by Applicable Law.

24. Agreements about New York Lien Law. I will receive all amounts lent to me by Lender subject to the trust fund provisions of Section 13 of the New York Lien Law. This means that I will: (a) hold all amounts which I receive and which I have a right to receive from Lender under the Note as a trust fund; and (b) use those amounts to pay for "Cost of Improvement" (as defined in Section 13 of the New York Lien Law) before I use them for any other purpose. The fact that I am holding those amounts as a trust fund means that for any building or other improvement located on the Property I have a special responsibility under the law to use the amount in the manner described in this Section 24.

25. Borrower's Statement Regarding the Property [check box as applicable].

☐ This Security Instrument covers real property improved, or to be improved, by a one or two family dwelling only.

☐ This Security Instrument covers real property principally improved, or to be improved, by one or more structures containing, in the aggregate, not more than six residential dwelling units with each dwelling unit having its own separate cooking facilities.

☐ This Security Instrument does not cover real property improved as described above.

BY SIGNING BELOW, I accept and agree to the promises and agreements contained in pages 1 through 19 of this Security Instrument and in any Rider signed by me and recorded with it.

Witnesses:

_____   _____ (Seal)
                                                                    - Borrower

_____   _____ (Seal)
                                                                    - Borrower

_____[Space Below This Line For Acknowledgment]_____

FEDERAL TRUTH-IN-LENDING DISCLOSURE STATEMENT
(THIS IS NEITHER A CONTRACT NOR A COMMITMENT TO LEND)

Loan Number: Date:

Creditor:

Address:

Borrower(s):

Address:

Disclosures marked with an "x" are applicable:

ANNUAL PERCENTAGE RATE	FINANCE CHARGE	Amount Financed	Total of Payments	☐ Total Sale Price
The cost of your credit as a yearly rate	The dollar amount the credit will cost you.	The amount of credit provided to you or on your behalf.	The amount you will have paid after you have made all payments as scheduled.	The total cost of your purchase on credit including your down-payment of $
%	$	$	$	$

PAYMENTS: Your payment schedule will be:

Number of Payments	Amount of Payment **	When Payments Are Due	Number of Payments	Amount of Payment **	When Payments Are Due	Number of Payments	Amount of Payment **	When Payments Are Due
		Monthly Beginning			Monthly Beginning			Monthly Beginning

☐ **DEMAND FEATURE:** This obligation has a demand feature.

☐ **VARIABLE RATE FEATURE:** Your loan contains a variable rate feature. Disclosures about the variable rate feature have been provided to you earlier.

PROPERTY INSURANCE: You may obtain fire and other hazard insurance from anyone you want that is acceptable to the Creditor.

NO OBLIGATION: You are not required to complete this agreement merely because you have received these disclosures or signed a loan application.

SECURITY: You are giving a security interest in:
☐ The goods or property being purchased   ☐ Real property you already own.

FILING FEES: $

LATE CHARGE: If payment is more than _____ days late, you will be charged _____% of the payment.

PREPAYMENT: If you pay off early, you
☐ may   ☐ will not   have to pay a penalty.
☐ may   ☐ will not   be entitled to a refund of part of the finance charge.

ASSUMPTION: Someone buying your property
☐ may   ☐ may, subject to conditions   ☐ may not   assume the remainder of your loan on the original terms.

See your contract documents for any additional information about nonpayment, default, any required repayment in full before the scheduled date and prepayment refunds and penalties.

☐ "e" means an estimate   ☐ all dates and numerical disclosures except the late payment disclosures are estimates.

Each of the undersigned acknowledge receipt of a complete copy of this disclosure. The disclosure does not constitute a contract or a commitment to lend.

_____   _____   _____   _____
Applicant   Date   Applicant   Date

_____   _____   _____   _____
Applicant   Date   Applicant   Date

_____   _____   _____   _____
Applicant   Date   Applicant   Date

** NOTE: Payments shown above do not include reserve deposits for taxes, assessments, and property or flood insurance.

SAMPLE

RECORDING REQUESTED BY

AND WHEN RECORDED MAIL DOCUMENT AND
TAX STATEMENT TO:

NAME

STREET
ADDRESS

CITY, STATE &
ZIP CODE

TITLE ORDER NO.   ESCROW NO.   SPACE ABOVE THIS LINE FOR RECORDER'S USE ONLY

GRANT DEED

APN:

The undersigned grantor(s) declare(s) _____
DOCUMENTARY TRANSFER TAX $
☐ computed on full value of property conveyed, or
☐ computed on full value less liens and encumbrances remaining at time of sale.
☐ Unincorporated Area   City of _____

FOR VALUABLE CONSIDERATION, receipt of which is hereby acknowledged, I (We)

hereby remise, release and grant to

the following described real property in the City of _____ ,County of _____
State of California, with the following legal description:

_____   _____
              Date

                                          _____

STATE OF _____

COUNTY OF _____

On _____ before me, _____,
              (Date)   (Name and title of the officer)

personally appeared _____, who proved to me on the basis of
                              (Name of person signing)
satisfactory evidence to be the person(s) whose name(s) is/are subscribed to the within instrument and acknowledged to me that
he/she/they executed the same in his/her/their authorized capacity(ies), and that by his/her/their signature(s) on the instrument the
person(s), or the entity upon behalf of which the person(s) acted, executed the instrument.

I certify under PENALTY OF PERJURY under the laws of the State of California that the foregoing paragraph is true and correct.

WITNESS my hand and official seal.

_____
        Signature of officer
                                                          (Seal)

MAIL TAX STATEMENT AS DIRECTED ABOVE

* There are various types of deed forms depending on each person's legal status. Before you use this form you many want to consult an
attorney if you have questions concerning which document form is appropriate for your transaction.

Monthly Income Worksheet

Figure Your Monthly Income

Your weekly pay $ _____   X 52 ÷ 12 $ _____
                         (take-home pay)   (monthly income)

or

Your twice-a-month pay $ _____   X 2 $ _____
                         (take-home pay)   (monthly income)

Your Monthly Take-home Pay $ _____

Figure Other Household Members' Monthly Income

Weekly pay $ _____   X 52 ÷ 12 $ _____
                         (take-home pay)   (monthly income)

or

Twice-a-month pay $ _____   X 2 $ _____
                         (take-home pay)   (monthly income)

Other Household Members' Take-home Pay $ _____

Other Monthly Income

Second job $ _____

Regular overtime $ _____

Public assistance $ _____

Child support $ _____

Pension $ _____

Social Security $ _____

Other $ _____

Total Other Monthly Income $ _____

Total Net Monthly Income $ _____

Monthly Expenses Worksheet

Housing
Rent or mortgage	$ _____
Heating *(gas or oil)*	$ _____
Electricity	$ _____
Water or sewage	$ _____
Telephones *(landlines and cell phones)*	$ _____
Renters or homeowners insurance	$ _____
(if not included in mortgage)	
Trash service	$ _____
Home maintenance and furnishings	$ _____
Cleaning supplies	$ _____
Lawn service	$ _____

Transportation
Gas	$ _____
Car payment	$ _____
Car insurance	$ _____
Car inspection	$ _____
Car repairs and maintenance	$ _____
License plates and registration fees	$ _____
Public transportation or taxi	$ _____
Parking and tolls	$ _____

Food
Groceries	$ _____
School lunches	$ _____
Work-related *(lunches and snacks)*	$ _____

Insurance
Health	$ _____
(medical and dental, if not payroll-deducted)	
Life	$ _____
Disability	$ _____

Medical
Doctor	$ _____
Dentist	$ _____
Prescriptions	$ _____

Childcare
Childcare or babysitters	$ _____
Child support or alimony	$ _____

Clothing
Clothing	$ _____
Laundry and dry cleaning	$ _____

Donations
Religious or charity	$ _____

Total Regular Monthly Expenses $ _____

Education
Tuition	$ _____
Books, papers and supplies	$ _____
Newspapers and magazines	$ _____
Lessons *(sports, dance, music)*	$ _____

Gifts
Birthdays	$ _____
Major holidays	$ _____

Personal
Barber or beauty shop	$ _____
Toiletries	$ _____
Children's allowances	$ _____
Tobacco products	$ _____
Beer, wine or liquor	$ _____

Entertainment
Movies, sporting events, concerts, etc.	$ _____
Video rentals	$ _____
Internet service	$ _____
Cable/satellite TV	$ _____
Restaurants and take-out meals	$ _____
Gambling and lottery tickets	$ _____
Fitness or social clubs	$ _____
Vacations/trips	$ _____
Hobbies or crafts	$ _____

Miscellaneous
Checking account and money order fees	$ _____
Pet care and supplies	$ _____
Postage	$ _____
Pictures and photo processing	$ _____
"Mad" money	$ _____

Debts
Student loan	$ _____
Credit card *(monthly minimum)*	$ _____
Credit card *(monthly minimum)*	$ _____
Credit card *(monthly minimum)*	$ _____
Medical bills	$ _____
Personal loan	$ _____

Other
Other	$ _____
Other	$ _____
Other	$ _____

Monthly Discretionary Income Worksheet

Figure Your Discretionary Income	Extra Money Each Month
Total Monthly Income	$ _____
Minus total regular monthly expenses	$ _____
Discretionary income *(Balance available to spend or save)*	$ _____

KEEPING TRACK OF YOUR SPENDING

The best way to find out where your money really goes is to begin keeping track of everything you and members of your household spend money on – from picking up the dry cleaning to getting shaving cream and greeting cards at the drug store to stopping for fast food to filling up at the gas station. Find a simple method of tracking that works for you, whether it be saving all receipts from purchases or giving each person a small notebook to write down expenditures.

The first step in taking command of your finances is to figure out where all the money is going. Only then can you redirect it for your benefit.

Look at your expenses weekly, and you may be surprised where the money goes. When you begin to develop a spending plan that includes saving for your goals, you can use your records to help you find places to cut your spending.

Monthly Spending Plan

This spending plan is broken down into the following types of expenses: fixed, periodic fixed, flexible and indebtedness. Depending on your situation, some expenses (for example, a cell phone) may be considered flexible rather than fixed. Be sure to adjust the categories to best reflect your needs and lifestyle.

	Monthly Expense	Budgeted Amount	Actual Spent	Difference
Fixed Expenses				
Housing	Rent or Mortgage			
	Heating (gas or oil)			
	Electricity			
	Telephones (landlines and cell phones)			
	Other:			
Transportation	Gas			
	Car Payment			
	Public Transportation or Taxi			
	Parking and Tolls			
	Other:			
Insurance	Health (medical and dental, if not payroll deducted)			
	Life			
	Disability			
	Other:			
Childcare	Childcare or Babysitters			
	Child Support or Alimony			
	Fixed Expenses Subtotal			
Periodic Fixed Expenses (divide annual payments by 12)				
Housing	Renters or Homeowners Insurance (if not included in mortgage)			
	Water or Sewage			
	Trash Service			
	Other:			
Transportation	Car Insurance			
	Car Inspection			
	Car Repairs and Maintenance			
	License Plates and Registration Fees			
	Other:			
	Periodic Fixed Expenses Subtotal			

	Monthly Expense	Budgeted Amount	Actual Spent	Difference
Flexible Expenses				
Food	Groceries			
	School Lunches			
	Work-Related (lunches and snacks)			
	Other:			
Housing	Home Maintenance and Furnishings			
	Cleaning Supplies			
	Lawn Care			
	Other:			
Medical	Doctor			
	Dentist			
	Prescriptions			
	Other:			
Savings	Emergency Fund			
	Down Payment Fund			
Clothing	Clothing			
	Laundry and Dry Cleaning			
	Other:			
Education	Tuition			
	Books, Papers and Supplies			
	Newspapers and Magazines			
	Lessons (sports, dance, music)			
	Other:			
Donations	Religious or Charity			
	Other (if not payroll deducted):			
Gifts	Birthdays			
	Holidays			
	Other:			
Personal	Barber or Beauty Shop			
	Toiletries			
	Children's Allowances			
	Tobacco Products			
	Beer, Wine, Liquor			
	Other:			

Source: CreditSmart by Freddie Mac

	Monthly Expense	Budgeted Amount	Actual Spent	Difference
Flexible Expenses Continued				
Entertainment	Movies, Sporting Events, Concerts, Theater, Etc.			
	Video Rentals			
	Internet Service			
	Cable/Satellite TV			
	Restaurants and Take-Out Meals			
	Gambling or Lottery Tickets			
	Fitness or Social Clubs			
	Vacations/Trips			
	Hobbies or Crafts			
	Other:			
Miscellaneous	Checking Account Fees, Money Order Fees, Etc.			
	Pet Care or Supplies			
	Postage			
	Pictures and Photo Processing			
	"Mad" Money			
	Other:			
	Flexible Expenses Subtotal			
Indebtedness Expenses				
Debt*	Student Loan			
	Credit Card (monthly minimum*)			
	Credit Card (monthly minimum)			
	Credit Card (monthly minimum)			
	Medical Bills			
	Personal Loan			
	Other:			
	Indebtedness Subtotal			
Total				
Total Monthly Expenses (fixed + periodic fixed + flexible + indebtedness)				
Income				
Total Monthly Net Income				
Additional Savings				
Amount Left Over for Savings (total monthly net income – total monthly expenses)				

*Although it is strongly recommended that you pay more than one monthly minimum payment due, lenders will use this amount when calculating monthly debt obligations.

www.ingramcontent.com/pod-product-compliance
Lightning Source LLC
Chambersburg PA
CBHW020336290526
45785CB00005B/2049